THE KENNEDY KURSE

Four Obvious Konnektions

I0135290

NIKKOLÒ

The Kennedy Kurse: Four Obvious Konnektions by Nikkolò

ISBN 978-1-64550-147-3 (Paperback)

CONTENTS

This book is part of a 2019 decalogue consisting of

- Sign of Times: Music Anthology and Lyric Analysis
- Hollywood Misogyny
- Beginners' Guide to the FED:
  Why it is Unique on our Planet
- The Kennedy Kurse: Four Obvious Konnektions
- Manichaeism and Satanic Child Abuse
- Progressive Intolerance: Last Stop Before Hitler
- Patriotic Ingenuousness
- Deism versus Theism:
  2-7 in the Scientific Arena of the 20th Century
- Feminine Feminist: A Missing Link Eluding Discovery
- The Snake: Three Millennia of Anti-Semitism

*Dedicated to the Happily Smiling JFK,
his Siblings and Parents*

INTRODUCTION

Government Conspiracy Blunders

When four events (in this book, the Kennedy assassinations) have plenty of possible causes (in this book, the mafias who ordered the assassinations), it is in principle a question of solving four separate problems. Equally generally, when something links those four events, there exists the possibility that the four problems are not separate, but together form a single problem.

The most ordinary common aspects of the assassinations one can think of, are (i) the surname "Kennedy", and (ii) the relatively short time span in which all four assassinations were carried out. Although these would hardly suffice to get police inspectors interested in the case, that is exactly what inspector Nikkolò pretends in this book. In order to make his point from the police perspective, therefore, Nikkolò should at least come up with a single "Client" (as he takes the liberty to nickname the single person who supposedly gave the four orders) and his motive.

Nikkolò is not a professional historian nor police inspector, but an ordinary scientist: the kind of which the universities are full of. Nikkolò believes that history and hard-core scientific disciplines have one thing in common: within their domain, general consensus among the professionals is possible, because there exists but one truth. As long as the professionals disagree, there exist but two theoretical options: either one of them knows and tells the truth, or neither of them do. It would be a contradiction in terms when two contradictory opinions were both true. The difference between history and hard-core sciences, however, is that establishing historical truth is infinitely more difficult than establishing scientific truth. The simple reason is that scientists can repeat experiments inquiring the behavior of nature whenever they want to, as their profession *is based on the belief* (or "scientific dogma") that the behavior of nature follows "general laws", valid throughout space and time. History, to the contrary, occurs only once, and in most cases, without adequate witnesses. The only way to get to historical truth as closely as possible, is gathering all reliable witnesses, and *calculating the odds* that a given set of presuppositions explains all their testimonies.

The average historian will certainly not recognize this as an historian's procedure. That is not really something one should be alarmed about. As a matter of fact, that very historian cannot explain the obvious lack of consensus among historians, even regarding the most thoroughly studied topics. Take the fall of the Western Roman Empire. More than enough testimonies. Yet, for every single interpretation, one can find an opposite one. These interpretations depend on the authors' religious and natural (economic, political, and social) beliefs.

Yet there do exist objective facts, extrinsic to the matter under study, which allow one to assess an historian's credibility. Whenever an historian is affiliated to an Institute, albeit the National Academy of Sciences, the author is not likely to write anything contradicting that Institute's creed, be it moral, political, financial, or jurisprudential. The nice words an Institute writes in its "Mission Statement" are always politically correct, and even if the Mission Statement made sense, there always is zero guarantee that any director of such an Institute behaves according to the Mission Statement. In case the choice were between the sack and accomplishing the Mission Statement, well, everybody knows what the director is going to do in 90% of the cases. With that same probability, the director of such an Institute would not allow employees to freely express their own thoughts whenever out of line with the owner(s) of the Institute.

Historical interpretations written by journalists are even more biased. One can best interpret those interpretations as what the owners of journals want the public to believe. In other words, media are mostly brainwashing machines, by the very fact that they are owned by someone, and today, in sharp contrast to last century, one does not own something without a clear profit.

Nikkolò does not pretend that journalists intentionally distort historical facts. No, a simple lack of honorability in one's sincere intention to find out the truth is enough. Unintentionally biased journalists simply keep digging until they find something that suits the Chief Editor's guidelines. This process is unconscious in most of the cases.

The advantage of journalism over academic studies, however, is that one can easily tell the bias, because the owners of the journals are publicly known. In contrast, one never knows for sure which people paid for *historic research*.

That is quite different in the field of medicine: there the bias is so obvious, that writers of a paper need to publish explicitly who provided them with the research funds. When a smoking industry has some research done on the medical effects of nicotine, one can weigh the conclusions accordingly. This is not such a simple issue in history. Exceptions do exist, of course, like David Robarge, CIA's chief historian. There the bias is candid, and one knows what parts of his stories are credible and what parts are meant to hide CIA's dirty laundry.

Nikkolò hereby declares that he did his research in his free time: Until the moment I write these words, I have received not a single penny for doing this research.[1]

Applying all the above theoretical wisdom to the four-Kennedy case, we will contrast our assumptions with the official ones, issued directly by the government. The latter are well formulated by the Wikipedia site on the Kennedy curse. Events that have been cited as evidence of the family's misfortunes include:

- 1941 — Rosemary Kennedy was often believed to have been intellectually disabled, and due to her severe mood swings and the worry that she would damage the Kennedy family reputation, her father, Joseph Sr., arranged in secret for her to undergo a lobotomy. The lobotomy instead left her unable to walk or speak well, and as a result, Rosemary remained institutionalized until her death in 2005.

---

1   I hope I will get funded in the future, though. But even then, I will make the sponsors known.

Rosemary's condition may have inspired her sister, Eunice, to initiate the Special Olympics in 1962.

- August 12, 1944 — Joseph P. Kennedy Jr. died when his plane exploded over East Suffolk, England, as part of Project Anvil during World War II.

- May 13, 1948 — Kathleen Cavendish, Marchioness of Hartington died in a plane crash in France.

- August 9, 1963 — Patrick Bouvier Kennedy died of infant respiratory distress syndrome two days after his premature birth (which itself occurred on the 20th anniversary of his father's World War II rescue). Jackie missed the funeral because she was still recovering from the C-section at Otis Air Force Base.

- November 22, 1963 — U.S. President John F. Kennedy was assassinated in Dallas, Texas by Lee Harvey Oswald. Oswald was shot dead by Jack Ruby two days later before he could stand trial. In 1964, the Warren Commission concluded that Oswald was the lone assassin. In 1979, the United States House Select Committee on Assassinations (HSCA) concluded that the assassination was the result of a conspiracy and that Oswald did not act alone.

- June 19, 1964 — U.S. Senator Ted Kennedy was involved in a plane crash in which one of his aides and the pilot were killed. Ted was pulled from the wreckage by fellow senator Birch Bayh and spent weeks in a hospital recovering from a broken back, a punctured lung, broken ribs, and internal bleeding.

- June 5, 1968 — U.S. Senator Robert F. Kennedy was assassinated by Sirhan Sirhan in Los Angeles immediately following his victory in the California Democratic presidential primary. Sirhan pleaded guilty to Robert's murder and is serving a life sentence at the Richard J. Donovan Correctional Facility.

- July 18, 1969 — In the Chappaquiddick incident, Ted Kennedy accidentally drove his car off a bridge on Chappaquiddick Island, which fatally trapped his 28-year-old passenger, Mary Jo Kopechne, inside. Ted pleaded guilty to a charge of leaving the scene of the accident causing personal injury. In his televised statement a week later, Ted stated that on the night of the incident he wondered "whether some awful curse did actually hang over all the Kennedys."

- April 25, 1984 — David A. Kennedy died of a cocaine and pethidine overdose in a Palm Beach, Florida hotel room.

- December 31, 1997 — Michael LeMoyne Kennedy died in a skiing accident in Aspen, Colorado.

- July 16, 1999 — John F. Kennedy Jr. died when his plane he was piloting, a Piper Saratoga, crashed into the Atlantic Ocean off the coast of Martha's Vineyard due to pilot error and spatial disorientation. His wife and sister-in-law were also on board and died.

- September 16, 2011 — Kara Kennedy died of a heart attack while exercising in a Washington, D.C. health club at age 51. Kara had reportedly suffered from lung cancer nine years earlier, but she had recovered after the removal of part of her right lung.

So what are the "official assumptions"? That all of these deaths are uncorrelated, and each has its own explanation. That is not written out explicitly, in order to fool the public. Very intelligent, indeed. In order to strengthen their claim of independence, more than half of the listed deaths are indeed totally uncorrelated:

- Rosemary Kennedy (1941, lobotomy)
- Kathleen Cavendish (1948, plane crash in France)
- Patrick Bouvier Kennedy (1963, IRDS two days after premature birth)
- David A. Kennedy (1984, cocaine and pethidine overdose)
- Michael LeMoyne Kennedy (1997, skiing accident)
- Kara Kennedy (2011, heart attack while exercising)

As far as I know, no single historian ever mentioned "suspect circumstances" in the above-mentioned deaths, let alone, suggested a "family curse": else, all families of this world would be cursed, thus emptying the word "curse" of its meaning. Now if there does exist a correlation between the deaths of the remaining four Kennedys —in the sense that they were ordered assassinations rather than natural deaths—, then this is just what a criminal organization would endeavor: to brainwash people into believing that all conspiracy theories, except the governmental one, are insane. The natural way to proceed, for such criminal organization, consists in producing enormous amounts of different and self-contradictory conspiracy theories. Especially when a plausible conspiracy theory appears, it should be delved under an avalanche of home-made conspiracy theories.

That is the reason that general disqualifications of conspiracy theories are quite realistic: most of those conspiracy theories are insane indeed. However, "most" is different from "all of them", and one would play the criminal organization's game by dismissing the very few *sane conspiracy theories*. Such lazy research behavior is called "throwing away the baby with the bathwater".

This book contains four "testimonial chapters" (one for each politically driven Kennedy assassination)[2], which collect a *biased selection* of testimonies, plus a fifth, conclusive chapter, containing Nikkolò's argument as well as his selection criteria used for the testimonies.

As a rule, for better legibility, all quoted passages are written using a different font as compared to the standard.

---

2   Whence excluding Joseph P. Kennedy Jr., Jack's eldest brother, who was killed in a plane explosion in 1944, during a WW II secret mission called "Anvil". From Joseph sr.'s extremely angry reaction to the dementing Roosevelt, it should be clear as to who gave the back-shot murder order. Mentioning the poor captain, who carried out the order by pushing the auto-destruction knob, is immaterial.

CHAPTER 1
John Fitzgerald (Jack) Kennedy

It is easy to imagine the CIA's frustration after their humiliation in the Bay of Pigs in Cuba (1961), followed by the missile crisis in 1962, during which the Kennedy brothers did their utmost to seek contact with the Russian President Nikita Sergeyevich Khrushchev, trying to pierce the cordon sanitaire of the Russian hardliners surrounding him. These two events are in principle imputable to JFK's "softness" on communists, or to his "pacifism", whatever one wishes to call it. In 1963, Kennedy signed the National Security Action Memorandum 263, which ordered withdrawing 1,000 military from Vietnam. It is very probable that Kennedy had in mind to withdraw the rest of the army from Vietnam upon re-election (in 1964). His speech in June of 1963 given before the American University of Washington D.C. was entitled "a strategy for peace". From his body language, and his emotions, one could easily notice this was not a mere happy-party speech. Notably, he commented that the United States were trying to approach the Soviet Union in order to begin a bilateral nuclear disarmament, and offer the Russians a promise that the US would never start a war against the Soviets. Plenty of reasons for military hardliners to get rid of a lousy democrat in supreme command, one might think.

1.1 Clint Eastwood Does Not Mind (But There Were 8 Shots)

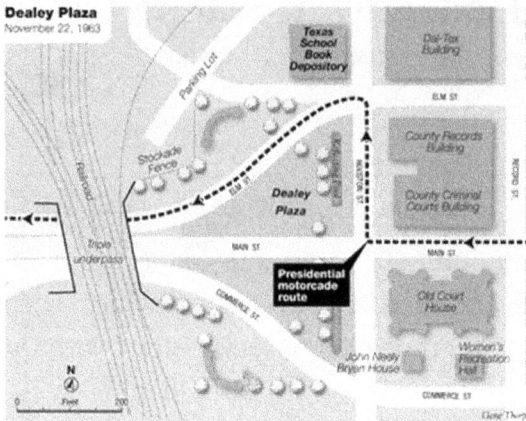

President John F. Kennedy was assassinated on November 22, 1963 on Dealey Plaza, Dallas, Texas. Randolph Robertson provides definitive proof that eight shots were fired from three different locations on the basis of an acoustic analysis. Of those eight shots, three impacted outside the presidential limousine. One hit Governor Connally, and four JFK.

Robertson's acoustic study was straightforward: he synchronized Zapruder's silent video footage with McLain's loose "DictaBelt" noise tape. This synchronization, *achieved with a precision of a few milliseconds*, not only counts eight shots and their multiple echoes, but also identifies *exactly* the three sites from where the shots originated (using standard, expanded-2D time-of-flight techniques).[3]

Just before the snipers' shot rain, Winston G. Lawson, CIA, ordered the motorcade to retreat. No more questions asked by the 9/11 commission, who apparently considered such a stupid (or conspiracy) order quite appropriate in those circumstances. The Commission did however show keen interest in Lawson's "personal feelings" at the time:

> "I thought the president did not appreciate motorized policemen around"

I thought? It would have been but a moderate joke, had this not truly happened. CIA Winston had better stick to the crystal clear German army wisdom: *Das Denken überlass den Pferden!*[4]

---

3   "Expanded 2D" means that the height dimension is only considered in a low-order approximation. The fifth shot from the Grassy Knoll was but slightly inclined, those from the Texas School Book Depository and the Dal-Tex Building somewhat more. If all shots had been perfectly horizontal, the mathematics would be simply 2D instead of 3D. Hence, "expanded 2D" is like a "near-3D" calculation.

4   "Leave the thinking to the horses!" This is an ironic command of superiors to privates who pretend to have an opinion. It explicitly says that, while in the army, privates are considered more stupid than horses. Of course, the whole issue is not about intelligence, but about blind obedience. The US army would not have it any different.

1.2 Jack Ruby

It is impossible that Vice-president Lyndon Baines Johnson ordered the assassination,[5] as his motivation would have been far too obvious. It would be equally ridiculous to believe a mob ordered the assassination. They knew well enough every President would persecute them, whether from the right or from the left. At most, LBJ and mobs participated on an anonymous mercenary level. The mere fact that the supposed shooter, Lee Harvey Oswald, was shot by Jack Ruby *before Oswald could defend himself in court* is enough of a proof that the President's assassination was a conspiracy.[6] As it also turns out that Jack Ruby died under very suspicious circumstances, the conspiracy is three-fold established. History writes the following:[7]

> On January 3, 1967, Jack Ruby, the Dallas nightclub owner who killed the alleged assassin of President John F. Kennedy, dies of cancer in a Dallas hospital. The Texas Court of Appeals had recently overturned his death sentence for the

---

5   This does not clear him from having cooperated directly. Remember his emotional shouting "those SOB's are never going to humiliate me again!" after the decisive CIA meeting
6   In https://www.youtube.com/watch?v=DJIoyMRe5EA& feature=youtu.be, it is clearly stated that, in a police interrogatory taken immediately after Kennedy's death, Oswald denies the Life picture was taken by his girlfriend, and clearly states it was a fake with his face pasted onto somebody else's body; he also kept repeating he was but a patsy.
7   https://www.history.com/this-day-in-history/jack-ruby-dies-before-second-trial

murder of Lee Harvey Oswald and was scheduled to grant him a new trial.

On November 24, 1963, two days after Kennedy's assassination, Lee Harvey Oswald was brought to the basement of the Dallas police headquarters on his way to a more secure county jail. A crowd of police and press with live television cameras rolling gathered to witness his departure. As Oswald came into the room, Jack Ruby emerged from the crowd and fatally wounded him with a single shot from a concealed .38 revolver. Ruby, who was immediately detained, claimed he was distraught over the president's assassination. Some called him a hero, but he was nonetheless charged with first-degree murder.

Jack Ruby, originally known as Jacob Rubenstein,[8] operated strip joints and dance halls in Dallas and had minor connections to organized crime. He also had a relationship with a number of Dallas policemen, which amounted to various favors in exchange for leniency in their monitoring of his establishments. He features prominently in Kennedy assassination theories, and many believe he killed Oswald to keep him from revealing a larger conspiracy. In his trial, Ruby denied the charge, maintaining that he was acting out of patriotism. In March 1964, he was found guilty and sentenced to death.

---

8   Other sources have Joseph

The official Warren Commission report of 1964 concluded that neither Oswald nor Ruby were part of a larger conspiracy, either domestic or international, to assassinate President Kennedy. Despite its seemingly firm conclusions, the report failed to silence conspiracy theories surrounding the event, and in 1978 the House Select Committee on Assassinations concluded in a preliminary report that Kennedy was "probably assassinated as a result of a conspiracy" that may have involved multiple shooters and organized crime. The committee's findings, as with the findings of the Warren Commission, continue to be widely disputed.

Of course, HSCA's preliminary conclusion that Kennedy was "probably assassinated as a result of a conspiracy" was heavily criticized, to wit, by the conspiracy itself. Make a list of all people criticizing HSCA's preliminary conclusion, and you will find exclusively conspirators or fools. As far as Ruby's distraught is concerned, it is quite obvious from his public statement given immediately after his shooting down Oswald (surrounded by Dallas cops, who were obviously ordered or blackmailed to let the miraculous disappearance of his testimony occur):

"Everything pertaining to what's happening has never come to the surface. The world will never know the true facts, of what occurred, my motives. The people that had so much to gain and had such an ulterior motive for putting me in the position I'm in, will never let the true facts come above board to the world."

Note the facial expressions of the police officers standing left behind the policeman wearing a light-colored suit leading Oswald, as if they were expecting the event to occur. The only startled look is that of the interviewer.

Ruby's quote is not that of ordinary hit men. The latter are proud of their professional skills; mentally sick people who operate like programmed computers. Their only bit of humanity conceals in their considering a game to elude the police, and an arrest as but a professional risk. Upon reading Ruby's quote again, one realizes that his is not ordinary hitman talking. He is rather crying out his frustration that his blackmailers are too mighty to let the truth emerge.

Ruby's death due to a pulmonary embolism, January 3 1967 in Parkland hospital, was not casual. Ruby's first death sentence did not come easily. Serious doubts had risen concerning Ruby's free will in killing Oswald, based on Ruby's own statements. After a long period in hospital, possibly due to the Client's trying to get rid of him, Ruby was granted a second trial. As is well known, Ruby died just before being able to appear. The simple conclusion would be that the Client (here used as a synonym for the group of people who ordered JFK's assassination) feared that Ruby might further unveil the Client. In 2008, David Reitzes informs in more detail about this conjecture, by literally quoting Ruby in his first trial:[9]

> On March 18, 1965, Jack Ruby's attorneys made an appearance in the United States District Court in Dallas, with Judge T. Whitfield Davidson presiding, seeking a writ of habeas corpus in order to insure that control of Ruby's whereabouts remain under the jurisdiction of the Federal Court and the Federal Marshall. Opposing arguments were also heard from the State, represented by Bill Alexander.
>
> The following afternoon Judge Davidson called a further hearing on the matter, As required by law, Ruby himself was brought before the judge, but none of Ruby's attorneys were prepared to attend. Ruby took advantage of the opportunity to speak without his attorneys present, interrupting the proceedings to make an unexpected appeal to the judge.
>
> "Your Honor, may I say something? I don't have any counsel here, your Honor, and I wish the courtesy of the Court to give me a chance to take the stand." Attorney Joe Tonahill was on hand, and, although he was not formally representing Ruby at the time, was allowed to preface Ruby's

---

9   http://www.jfk-online.com/ruby-conspiracy.html

statements with some remarks. Tonahill sought to inform the Court that psychiatrist L. J. West had sworn an affidavit stating that "Jack Ruby was insane, and highly susceptible to delusions and suspicions, and a complete paranoid." Dr. West had demonstrated, Tonahill said, that Ruby's condition necessitated the presence of an attorney to represent him. He also insisted that Ruby's mental illness was primarily responsible for his own removal from Ruby's defense team. Judge Davidson allowed Ruby to speak, however. "I will permit him to stand where he is," without requiring Ruby to be sworn in, "and he may give the Court any statement he may care to give." Ruby wasted no time whatsoever. "This is the most tragic thing in the history of the world," he announced. "One of the most tragic conspiracies in the world," he declared. "I will get on the stand and speak with tears in my heart because of such a terrible conspiracy which is combined against me." This is it, ladies and gentlemen: the moment we've all been waiting for. Jack Ruby is about to blow the lid off one of the most heinous conspiracies of all time. "What Mr. Tonahill has said is a total lie", Ruby continued. "That goes from the contract I signed, I never did sign a contract with him. It has been a conspiracy between him and the District Attorney, [attorney] Phil Burleson and Joe Tonahill, to convince the public that Jack Ruby is insane. Now, your Honor, you have had many a person appear before you pleading their case. If I am a person who sounds insane at this time, then the rest of the world is crazy. I say this with choking in my heart and tears in my eyes. The most tragic thing happened that Sunday morning when I went down that ramp. I happened to be there for a purpose which is going to be the most tragic thing that ever happened in this world. [Lengthy description of Ruby's succession of attorneys omitted.] At 10:15, I left my apartment, and the story was out that this person [Oswald] was supposed to leave the jail at 10:00 AM. I received a call from a young girl [Karen Carlin, one of Ruby's strippers] who wanted some money. [Because Ruby had closed his club for the weekend, out of respect for the slain President, Carlin was unable to pay her rent.][10] I went to the Western Union, which was coincidental, and prior to that, I will admit [I'd read] a letter [that] was written to Caroline [Kennedy — actually an editorial in the November 24, 1963, edition of the Dallas Times Herald] which broke my heart. This letter was written to Caroline telling her how awfully sorry I was for her. And another situation [in another article], there was something about a trial [Mrs. Kennedy expected to return to Dallas for Oswald's trial]. Don't ask me what took place, and that triggered me off that Sunday morning. I accepted the call at 10:15 and went down to the Western Union and parked my car across the street, and took off to

---

10   Warren Commission Report, pp. 348-56

transact my business. At 11:17 I walked, I don't say it was premeditated, but never prior to Sunday morning, I never made up my mind what to do. From 11:17 until later, I was guilty of a homicide. Which must be the most perfect conspiracy in the history of the world that a man was going to accept a call and came from his apartment down to the Western Union. If it had been three seconds later I would have missed this particular person [Oswald]. I guess God was against me. I left the Western Union and it took about three and a half minutes to go to the bottom of the ramp. I didn't conspire or sneak in to do these things, I am telling you. If they had said, 'Jack, are you going down now?' that would make some conspiracy on me. I left the Western Union and it was a fraction of a second until that tragic act happened. Now, it seems all these circumstances were against me. I had a great emotional feeling for our beloved President and Mrs. Kennedy, or I never would have been involved in this tragic crime, that was completely reverse from what my emotional feeling was." Ruby returned to the subject of his numerous attorneys and how he felt they had mistreated him and mishandled his defense: "As far as Joe Tonahill is concerned, he doesn't care what happens to me, nor does Phil Burleson, and I am not saying this just to make the headlines, I am not remembering this from rehearsal, I am speaking word-for-word, that I know what took place. And I am like the stupid idiot, that loved this country so much, and I felt so sorry for Mrs. Kennedy when she was standing on that plane with blood on her dress, and they were bringing the casket back with our beloved President, and now I am going to [go] down in history as the most despicable person that ever lived. If I am able to use this little oratory on you, as I am doing, if I have that capability, looking at you and telling this courtroom a slight fraction of a lie then I am a genius. Thank you."*11*

Contrary to what some people would like to believe, whenever Ruby had a chance to describe the "conspiracy" against him, the "conspiracy" ultimately turned out to be a plot to falsely implicate him in the Kennedy assassination — not exactly what conspiracy theorists would seem to have in mind.*12*

[S]ome persons are accusing me falsely of being part of the plot, a plot to silence Oswald," Ruby told the Warren Commission in 1964. "[T]he people that have the power here already have me [portrayed] as the accused assassin of our beloved President."*13* He pleaded for a chance to reassure President Johnson in person that he was not part of any such plot, and lamented that LBJ

---

11 Elmer Gertz, Moment of Madness: The People vs. Jack Ruby (Chicago: Follett Publishing Co., 1968), pp. 174-189
12 This is a confusing paragraph, as Reitz fails to mention what conspiracy theory he is talking about. Most of those theories are circulated by the conspiracy itself, of course, though I fear Reitz has no clue.
13 Warren Commission Hearings Vol. V, p. 209

"has been told, I am certain, that I was part of a plot to assassinate the President."[14] (...)[15] In a letter from prison to his brother Earl, Ruby wrote, "You must believe what I've been telling you for the past two and a half years. If you only would have believed me all along you would have found some way to check out what I said. You would have saved Israel, but now they are doomed, because they think the U.S. are for them, but they are wrong because Johnson wants to see them slaughtered and tortured. Egypt is making believe they are an ally of Russia, that is only to fool Russia and the rest of the world. The Arabs are going to overrun Israel. They are going to get help both from Russia and the U.S. It's too late now to do anything, and we are all doomed." "They are torturing children here. If you only would believe what I'm telling you. Phil [Burleson] was in on the conspiracy all along, and he was very instrumental in the frame-up they planned, [claiming] that I was in on the assassination of the President."[16]

Ruby's defense in court is, in my view, a strong pointer to the fact there *was indeed* a conspiracy, with the obligated mandating criminal organization, whose commander-in-

---

14 Warren Commission Hearings Vol. V, p. 211.
15 Some more irrelevant nonsense of Reitz' own making, which I am not discussing here. I only comment on authentic quotes by Ruby.
16 Elmer Gertz, Moment of Madness: The People vs. Jack Ruby (Chicago: Follett Publishing Co., 1968), p. 472

chief Nikkolò will call "the Client" throughout the book: he is the supposed Master Mind who does all the thinking, and holds the *motive* for the criminal organization's operations.

This "Client" tried it all to misrepresent Lee Harvey Oswald as a disoriented communist (he was a CIA agent once sent to Russia), and Jack Ruby as out of his mind. However, Oswald's replies to the immediate police hearings were all but disoriented, and Ruby's defense in court proves that he had full control over his wits. His own "court defense" did everything possible to silence him, all the way down to begging the judge, but the latter harshly overruled them, clearly irritated by their obvious intent to silence Ruby.

Of course, there will always be people who consider Ruby's defense as confused. So it would seem to me, too, as long as there were no single indication of conspiracy. But Ruby speaks out the word "conspiracy" loud and clear himself, under oath, in court! These over-rational people really amuse me. Specifically, I would like to know how convincingly they would present their defense under similar circumstances. I am afraid most of them would not reach it beyond pissing their pants.

1.3 Trump's Fake "Full-Release"

In October 2017, 2,800 files about the 1963 murder were made public for the first time, bringing to the fore revelations that an alleged Cuban intelligence officer met Lee Harvey Oswald in Mexico City, and praised his shooting ability, and that the Soviet spy agency KGB believed then-Vice President Lyndon Johnson may have conspired to assassinate Kennedy.

On April 26, in compliance with the deadline set by President Trump in October 2017, the National Archives released 19,045 additional documents from the JFK assassination files.[17] Despite a promise to release all archives on JFK on April 26, 2018, the Trump administration is still withholding material in the JFK Assassination archive for extra review. The excuse, this time, is "identifiable national security, law enforcement, and foreign affairs concerns," according to a White House memo. The president said he was ordering agencies to "rereview each of the redactions over the next three years," and set a deadline for further release of documents of October 26, 2021.

Whatever.

This once again confirms the existence of Mr. Client. What is quite worrying, though, is his enormous political influence.

Revelations since October 2018 about JFK's assassination

After that initial release in October, the National Archives made four additional releases in November and December,[18] totaling around 35,000 files published in

---

17 https://www.history.com/news/final-jfk-files-assassination-documents-release
18 https://www.archives.gov/research/jfk/2017-release

2017, many of which were partially or mostly redacted. One of the more intriguing disclosures related to Oswald's attempts to get a Soviet or Cuban visa during his visit to Mexico City[19] (which the CIA thought might mean he was planning ahead for a quick escape after murdering Kennedy).

Meanwhile, dozens of other memos shed light on the controversy surrounding James Angleton,[20] the CIA's chief of counter-espionage, who did not tell the Warren Commission about the agency's involvement in an effort to overthrow or kill Cuban dictator Fidel Castro. His failure to do so has fueled later conspiracy theories concerning a CIA cover-up of Cuban involvement in JFK's murder.

Another batch of documents revealed the doubts CIA officials had about the testimony of Yuri Nosenko,[21] a former KGB agent who claimed that the spy agency made no attempt to recruit Oswald while he was in the Soviet Union.

This stinks "conspiracy" from all its pores, though not one organized by 4 Arab illiterate children, but by a criminal organization much wealthier than the US.

---

19 https://www.archives.gov/files/research/jfk/releases/104-
    10436-10084.pdf
20 https://www.usatoday.com/story/news/politics/2017/11/13/
    jfk-files-controversy-surrounding-cia-counterspy-chief-fed-
    assassination-conspiracies/857616001/
21 https://www.archives.gov/files/research/jfk/releases/180-
    10131-10324.pdf

1.4 Madeleine Duncan Brown Blows a Whistle on the JFK Assassination, 22 Nov 2006[22]

The night before the Kennedy assassination, Clint Williams Murchison Sr. (a Texas-based oil magnate) organized a briefing to inform LBJ (Vice President, future democrat 36th President), J. Edgar Hoover (CIA), John Jay McCloy (banker from the Chase Manhattan Bank), Richard Milhous Nixon (ex-Vice President, future republican 37th President), Haroldson Lafayette Hunt (an oil magnate) and his gay friend John Currington, George Brown (a military business tycoon, interested in prolonging the Vietnam war), Amon G. Carter jr. (a mining tycoon), Earle Cabell (Mayor of Dallas, congressman, brother of Charles Pearre Cabell, Deputy Director of CIA, fired by JFK), Harry S. Truman (democrat 33rd President), John Bowden Connally Jr. (ex-Navy, Governor of Texas, from 1971 Treasury Secretary under Richard Nixon, presided over the removal of the U.S. dollar from the gold standard, an event known as the Nixon shock), George Washington Owen (employee of Clint Murchison jr.), Cliff Carter (LBJ's right hand),

---

22 https://www.youtube.com/watch?v=79lOKs0Kr_Y (short extract) or https://youtu.be/POmdd6HQsus (long)

Malcolm E Wallace (economist for the United States Department of Agriculture), Carlos Marcello (the powerful Mafia chief of New Orleans), and Joseph Francis Civello (leader of the Dallas mob).

Late Madeleine Duncan Brown

Exiting that conference half-way, LBJ grabbed his mistress, Madeleine Duncan Brown, by the arm and told her emotionally that "after tomorrow, those SOB's will never embarrass me again: that's no threat, that's a promise".

1.5 *The Backyard Photos of Lee Harvey Oswald Are Fakes!*

by John Kays, May 9, 2009[23]

I am still pained today by the slaying of John Kennedy in downtown Dallas, all those years ago. I began to study this case in earnest in the mid-1970s, when so many anomalies in the investigation could be observed. The 'Luminosity of Truth' is not always quite as clear as we would prefer. The backyard photos of Lee Oswald, taken casually by Marina on March 31st, 1963, have always been a great source of confusion in this case. The best explanation of these mysterious photos, that I have been able to find, is provided by Jack White, a photographic expert from Fort Worth.

When questioned by Captain Will Fritz, and shown the incriminating backyard photo, Lee said that it was a fake, and that his head was pasted on to someone else's body, in order to frame him up for the killing of the President.[24]

---

23 https://newsblaze.com/usnews/national/the-backyard-photos-of-lee-harvey-oswald-are-fakes_9208/

24 https://youtu.be/DJIoyMRe5EA

Fake: the Forged Photograph that Framed Lee Harvey Oswald is the video about the findings of Jack White. It was first broadcast in 1990 and was produced by Jim Marrs, a JFK expert.

Supposedly, two photos and one negative were found at Ruth Paine's house in Irving. Most puzzling though, is the fact that detective Gus Rose of the Dallas Police Department says he found two negatives. Another mysterious tidbit is that the dark shirt and pants that Lee wore at the photo-shoot were never retrieved from the Ruth Paine home?

In 1967 another photo emerged from some stored possessions of George de Mohrenchildt's, a friend of Oswald's with CIA connections. This was a higher quality photo, that seemed to have been taken with a higher quality camera. It had a black border, which indicates, according to Jack White, that it was taken from the negative, which was lost very early on in the investigation. On the back of the photo the words "Hunter of Fascists Ha Ha Ha" is written. Both Lee and Marina have been eliminated by handwriting experts as the writers of this odd slogan.

In 1976 a third photo was found at the home of the widow of Roscoe White, a shadowy Dallas policeman who may have been involved with the assassination conspiracy. His story is more revealed in a second video; The Many Faces of Lee Harvey Oswald, which I will link below also. Moreover, Jim Marrs interviewed Robert and Pat Hester, who are dead now, but they had worked in a photographic lab (I do not know the exact connection of the lab to the assassination). They were shown the photos by the FBI on the night of the assassination, one day before they were supposedly discovered at Ruth Paine's home. One shot was just of the background with the staircase at the famous Neely house (I have visited it before). Lee wasn't in the picture!

Some serious problems exist with these photos (Warren Exhibits 133 A, 133 B, and 133 C), as clarified in Fake. In 133 A, the famous Life Magazine photo, no one has ever been able to duplicate the hand gripping of the rifle, as Lee did. Also, the right shoulder slumps, as you can clearly see. These are signs of sloppy touch up work. Most troublesome, is the fact that there are no fingernails on the right hand, the hand holding the leftist newspaper The Militant. Puzzling also, is the fact that shadows fall in different positions, even though the snapshots were taken very close together in time.

There are many other riddles and people should take a look at all of them closely. I will just tell you of a few of them, then I am sure your curiosity will sweep you off your feet, and you will put a magnifying glass down on this pristine image. The wristwatch seen on Oswald's left arm in 133 B was never retrieved. How could this be? The Imperial Reflex Camera of Oswald, purportedly used by Marina to take the photos, was not found until December 8th, by Lee's brother Robert. Why was this?

The rifle size is too big for Lee's body. The Warren Commission tried to cover this up by publishing a later ad of the rifle. The rifle in the National Archives is 40 inches in length. The rifle ordered by Lee was a 36 inch rifle. Also, in the photo the rear end of the telescopic scope is missing? More evidence of doctoring, I will suggest.

The most fascinating facts for me, are the evidence regarding the face. The face in this picture shows a flat chin, yet it is known fact that Oswald had a sharp, cleft chin. Jack White detected water spots on the negative. You can just about see the line where the face has been pasted onto the torso. White conducted a test where he placed a red transparency of 133 B over a blue transparency of 133 A. The faces exactly lined up. This is impossible, if they were two unique photographs? Therefore, the same head was grafted onto the two photos.

The neck (in 133 A and B) is very much thicker than Oswald's real neck. He was known to have a 14 1/2 inch collar; however, the person in this image has a 16 inch collar, a 1 1/2 inch difference. This is clearly not Lee's body! Jack White is certain that the background used was the same building block to create the various composites. Clever cropping and tilting of the easel were used to project the illusion of different shots. Please look for these details when you watch the video.

He proves that the same background was used. It is an impossibility for the camera to be in the exact same position, unless a tripod had been employed.

The two official investigations of the backyard photos were both rather shallow. The Warren Commission tried to do a reenactment of the scene, and left the head off in their print published in the Warren Report! Why did they do this? Their main proof that the photos are genuine, is that the markings on the negatives were legitimately from the Imperial Reflex Camera. But White figured out how the conspirators pulled this off! They first built the composite in a sophisticated laboratory using a much better camera, then they photographed the photograph with the Imperial Reflex Camera, so that the negative would have matching forensics to the camera. The House Select Committee on Assassinations, the second major investigatory body, conducted Pinrose Distance Statistics, where they would compare body measurements of known Oswald photos with the controversial shots of Lee in these suspicious poses. However, in their final report, they left out important statistical data, that did not jive. The essential chin measurements would have spoiled their report, so they were omitted!

Jack White was able to account for the fact that one face has a frown and one a smile, by the use of touchup, just on the lips. Everything else in the face is identical, an impossibility, when you consider all of the muscles in your face! Mister White actually models these scientific facial characteristics, by mimicking a smile and a frown in the video!

And so there you have it, a clever forgery was pulled off by using graphics blenders in some sophisticated facility. Jack White has unveiled this forgery very convincingly, from what I can tell, and the implication of this is indeed chilly ... indeed most nefarious. A conspiracy to frame Lee Oswald as the sole shooter of John Kennedy was concocted, and the infamous backyard photos were an integral part of this plot. Jim Marrs thanks Jack White for his groundbreaking work at the end of the video, and urges citizens to look beyond the government experts for the truth.

I fear that very few Americans even know anything about this clever fabrication of these images of Oswald; it truly looks like they were manipulated in a photographic lab of a very high caliber. I hope that my humble article will reach a great amount of people, and that they will begin to view this video in numbers; it contains razor-sharp explanations for these enigmas of the camera, this flagrant trickery that fooled 'We the People'. Most certainly they then will come to the same conclusions that I have come to: that President Kennedy was slain on the 'Streets of Dallas' by a cache of vengeful powerbrokers (Right Wing Extremists) who found it a necessity to rid themselves of a liberal JFK, and his progressive policies, that really transformed our country and put it on a better path.

1.6 *JFK Head Wound Forensics*

by Joe Giambrone, October 23, 2013[25]

For the 50th anniversary of the assassination, I am involved in a research project on the best evidence concerning what happened, and what did not happen. The head shot is one small part of a large tangled web. Oswald was known to US intelligence for a long time prior to 1963. With the Cuban covert operations, the Bay of Pigs incident, JFK's firing of Allen Dulles and basically dismantling the CIA's action capabilities, we have a clear motive for wanting him removed from power.

---

25 https://politicalfilm.wordpress.com/2013/10/23/jfk-head-wound-forensics/

- Controversy stems from whether the frontal damage is an entrance wound or an exit wound.
- Also controversy surrounds whether the bullet damage reached the very back of the skull, "occipital" region.
- The "flap" is apparently a dislodged piece of scalp that originally covered over the frontal area head wound.

Eyewitness Marilyn Sitzman[26] to JFK shooting describes frontal wound as bullet entrance wound [transcript of tape recording[27]]:

Thompson: Where on the side of the head did that shot appear to hit?
Sitzman: I would say it'd be above the ear and to the front.
Thompson: In other words, if one drew a line vertically upward from the tip of the ear, it would be forward of that line?
Sitzman: Yeah.

---

26 The woman who held Abraham Zapruder steady while he was filming the motorcade
27 http://mcadams.posc.mu.edu/sitzman.txt

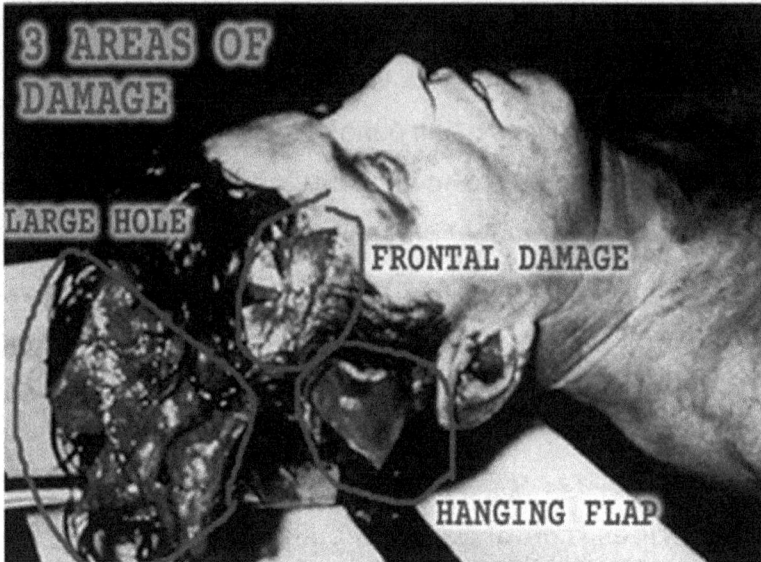

Autopsy Photograph credited to
Dr. Groden (Bethesda Naval Hospital)[28]

Thompson: It would then mean the left ... back of the temple, but on the side of the head, back of the temple?

Sitzman: Between the eye and the ear.

Difficulty In Analyzing The Evidence

The House Select Committee on Assassination in 1979 acknowledged discrepancies between descriptions of Kennedy's head wounds by the Dallas doctors versus Bethesda autopsy personnel:[29] "The description of the size and

---

28 http://commons.wikimedia.org/wiki/File:JFK_autopsy.jpg
29 http://mcadams.posc.mu.edu/autopsy2.txt

location of the President's head wounds, for example, by eyewitnesses at Parkland Hospital differed dramatically from the testimony of the autopsy doctors and the account set forth in the Warren Report.(195) More recently, the panel of medical experts convened by then-Acting Attorney General Ramsey Clark described Kennedy's head entrance wound as approximately 10 centimeters higher than the location reported by the Warren Commission."

[Nikkolò: Now Follow 4 frames of the Zapruder film, without comments by the author; any comments are mine].*30*

---

30 http://www.assassinationresearch.com/zfilm/.
Author's Comment: On the four stills shown below, one clearly observes JFK's head being tilted forward. This tilt was provoked by an earlier shot, shot from behind (i.e. one of the tall buildings). The first shot caused the First Lady to bend over to JFK. The four frames are so close in time, that *Jacqueline's head does not move an inch* on these four frames. This shot had JFK's head move from his normal position (at the back), to the extreme forward position, colliding with the seat occupied by Texas Governor John Connally. James Files' lead-filled bullet entered from the front, having JFK's head bounce back from the forward prostration to the extreme back. From the here adduced references one may read exactly how and when the Zapruder film was manipulated by the CIA that very weekend. In reality, frame 314 (the first one) should be 316. Two frames were cut for the purpose of hiding from the public the obvious truth that the eighth bullet came from the front, and splattered JFK's skull and brains all over the place, *with a clear ejection of brain matter towards the back.* leaving a diameter 8" exit hole..

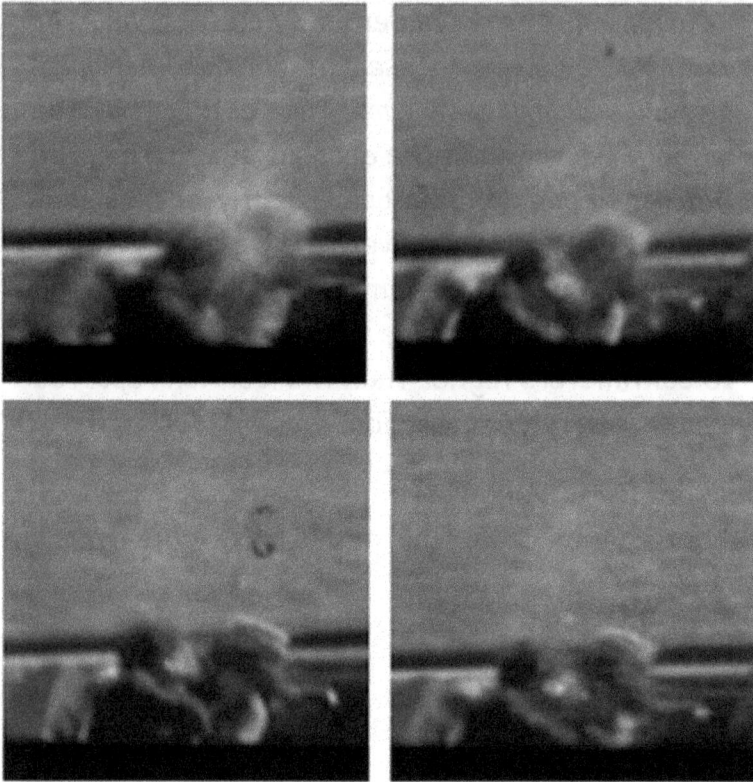

Manipulated Zapruder frames 314-318. In frame 314 JFK's head moves backward with a speed of 20" per second, whereas in the frames before 313 JFK's head was moving forward with half that speed, pounding JFK's head onto Connally's seat. Since the camera has a frame rate of 18.3 frames per second, JFK's head underwent an acceleration, during one frame's time (55 milliseconds), of 30" per second per 55 milliseconds, or 545" per square second. The smoothest possible way to realize this sudden acceleration is to blow his brains literally off. The CIA decided to fool the public, and hide the eighth shot for the public, in order to brainwash the American people into continuing their winter sleep.

Consequently, JFK's head moves backward with a velocity of 20" per second. If this was the result of a back shot, then I am decidedly a goose.

Bell & Howell Zoomatic movie camera used to shoot the Zapruder film

[end of Nikkolò's comments]

Head X-Ray Evidence

Only two views have been shown to public. Severe fractures visible at rear, *possible cosmetic reconstruction.*

Jerrol Custer, a JFK autopsy X-ray technician (evening of Nov. 22, 1963), told author David Lifton that the wound in the skull was posterior [at the back] in the skull and said that "he exposed, and returned to the morgue, X- rays showing that the rear of the President's head was blown off." (Best Evidence , p. 620)

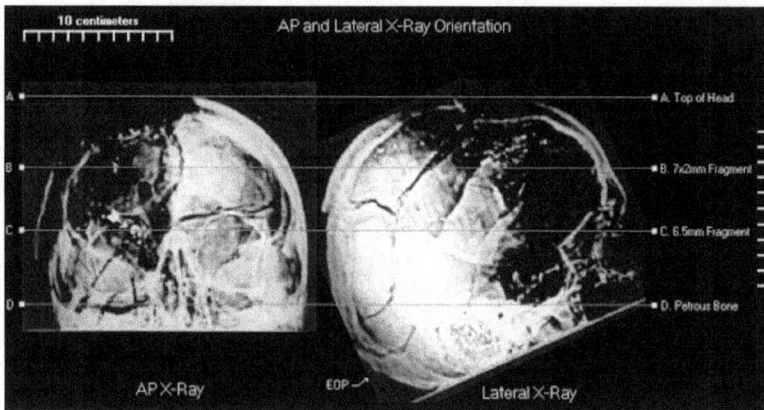

10 centimeters	AP and Lateral X-Ray Orientation
A	A. Top of Head
B	B. 7x2mm Fragment
C	C. 6.5mm Fragment
D	D. Petrous Bone
AP X-Ray EOP	Lateral X-Ray

X-Ray Technician Claims Images Are Forgeries

The extant X-rays show no such thing. May 29, 1992 and November 18, 1993 press conferences Custer repeated his consistent claim that the current X-rays are forgeries. (Reuters wire service, reported in: Duffy JP, Ricci VL, The Assassination of John F. Kennedy, New York, 1992, Thunder's Mouth Press, p. 142.)

JERROL CUSTER was an X-Ray Technician at the JFK autopsy, Assassination Records Review Board Deposition, October 28, 1997:[31]

Q: Did you see any reconstruction of the body at all by morticians?

CUSTER: I remember **when I looked into the skull – I remember seeing an apparatus in there.**

---

31 http://www.aarclibrary.org/publib/jfk/arrb/medical_
    testimony/pdf/Custer_10-28-97.pdf

Q: Could you describe the apparatus that was in the skull.

CUSTER: It was non-human. It had – **I'm not sure if it was metallic or plastic...**

...CUSTER: Their basic thing was "We're looking for shells, bullets, fragments." They weren't looking to what caused it? How was it done? What was the tracing – what was the path of the bullet?

Q: How was it that you came to the impression that what they were doing was looking for bullet fragments?

CUSTER: That was plain and simple. They come right out and said, "You're taking X-Rays for bullets."

CUSTER: The head was so unstable, due to the – the fractures. The fractures were extremely numerous. It was like somebody took a hardboiled egg and just rolled it in her hand. ...And every time we picked the head up, you could feel it. This part of the head would come out; this part of the head would be in. And it was just – The only thing holding it together was the skin.

During the autopsy, Custer also said that Dr. Ebersole, his commanding officer, told him that he had brought in JFK skull fragments, which had arrived from Dallas. "High-ranking people had talked to him. **And he suggested to me that everything I see from now on, I should forget."** (ARRB deposition, p146)

The HSCA addressed the possibility of fraudulent X-Rays in 1979.[32]

Their conclusion was to simply assume that 14 of the "Parkland personnel could be mistaken…"

HSCA uses a number of X-Ray experts to authenticate that the images are of Kennedy, however the report includes **no mention at all of JERROL CUSTER**, the man who actually took at least one set of known X-Ray images of President Kennedy that night.

Another finding of HSCA:

"FBI agents Silbert and O'Neill referred to "surgery" of the head area being evident when the body arrived for the autopsy"

GARY AQUILAR M.D., 1994 COMPILATION OF MEDICAL WITNESSES[33]

These eyewitnesses said that JFK's frontal head damage was likely an entry wound, and/or the rear head wound was an exit wound:

Dallas Parkland Hospital

Gary Aquilar paraphrases DOCTOR ROBERT MCLELLAND, who "…made clear that he thought the rear wound in the skull was an exit wound (WC-V6:35,37)."

RONALD COY JONES: was a senior General Surgery resident physician at Parkland Hospital: "…described "what appeared to be an exit wound in the posterior portion of the skull". (WC-

---

32 http://mcadams.posc.mu.edu/autopsy2.txt
33 http://www.assassinationweb.com/ag6.htm

V6:56)[34]   Asked   to   speculate: "...the   only speculation that I could have as far as to how this could occur with a single wound would be that it would enter the anterior neck and possibly strike a vertebral body and then change its course and exit in the region of the posterior portion of the head." (WC.V.6:56)" "In January, 1983 he told David Lifton, "If you brought him in here today, I'd still say he was shot from the front.""

PAUL PETERS MD: "...the only answer we could think (of) was perhaps the bullet had gone in through the front [of the neck], hit the bony spinal column, and exited through the back of the head, since a wound of exit is always bigger than a wound of entry."

CHARLES   CRENSHAW   MD: "...From   the damage I saw, there was no doubt in my mind that the bullet had entered his head through the front, and as it surgically passed through his cranium, the missile obliterated part of the temporal and all the parietal and occipital lobes before it lacerated the cerebellum." (JFK: Conspiracy of Silence, p. 86)"

ROBERT GROSSMAN MD: Never testified to Warren Commission, not mentioned by other doctors as being present. ""He (Grossman) said that he saw two large holes in the head, as he told the (Boston) Globe, and he described a large hole squarely in the occiput, far too large for a bullet

---

34 http://www.assassinationweb.com/ag6.htm

entry wound...". (HT-I Groden and Livingstone, p. 51)-& also "Duffy & Ricci, The Assassination of John F. Kennedy-A Complete Book of Facts, p. 207-208.)"

NURSE DIANA HAMILTON BOWRON: "When asked her opinion of the nature of the defect in the rear of the skull, Bowron told Livingstone, "Well, to me it was an exit hole."[35]

Livingstone asked, "Did you see any entry hole in the back of the head?". "I assumed and I still do that that was an exit wound." Bowron answered."

GREG AKIN MD, Anesthesiologist: 'I assume that the right occipitoparietal region was the exit.'"[36]

Bethesda Naval Base

JAN GAIL RUDNICKI: Dr. Boswell's lab assistant on the night of the autopsy: "...from the ear back, the scalp was either gone or definitely destroyed in that area.....it would look more like it was an exit than an entrance."

JERROL CUSTER: "Which tells you again, you had to have a king-size force coming anterior to posterior [front to back]. Everything seemed like it was just pushed backwards. This whole area blew out." (ARRB) ..."Here's another thing

---

35 Livingstone, Killing the Truth, p. 192
36 Lifton, BE, p.317

too, that shows this is more than likely – I'd say 80 to 90 percent – entry wound." [indicating front wound over sinuses] (ARRB)[37]

Many forensic witnesses speculated that the bullet entered from the rear, top or front, leading to conflicting descriptions.

Expert witness claims two bullets hit president's head:

RANDOLPH H. ROBERTSON M.D. examined x-rays of Kennedy's head and testified to the Congress, November 17, 1993.[38]

"We are left to wonder why this **obvious evidence of a second impact** was not recognized by the original autopsy team. We may also ask why the largest bullet fragment present on these x-rays was not recovered the night of the autopsy. It is my belief that this fragment was dropped out of the evidentiary chain because it was related to the second bullet which struck President Kennedy's head originating from the Grassy Knoll area."

However, Robertson's article on the 2nd head injury bullet was rejected by Radiology Journal, whose reviewer stated:

"The two prints included with the manuscript **are very difficult to interpret**. Therefore, I believe prudent pathologists would be very

---

37 http://www.aarclibrary.org/publib/jfk/arrb/medical_
testimony/pdf/Custer_10-28-97.pdf
38 http://mcadams.posc.mu.edu/robertsn.txt

hesitant to make a firm statement regarding precise locations, or beginning and ending point of fracture lines based on these images."

Recollections Have Changed Over Time

Some doctors have changed their statements since testifying to the Warren Commission, and others have been challenged as to what they had said. Example:

Anesthesiologist MARION JENKINS[39] has told conflicting stories of the cerebellum hanging out of JFK's wound and also a claim of a wound on the **left** temporal area which is not seen in the autopsy.

Additional Info On Throat Wound

Parkland Hospital Press Conference, Dallas Doctors First Statements, Press Conference[40] At Parkland Memorial Hospital, Dallas, November 22, 1963, 2:16 P.M. Cst

"Question-Doctor, describe the entrance wound. You think from the front in the throat?

DR. MALCOM PERRY- The wound appeared to be an entrance wound in the front of the throat; yes, that is correct."

---

39 http://www.assassinationweb.com/ag6.htm
40 http://mcadams.posc.mu.edu/press.htm

1.7 Where There's Smoke There's Fire

by Joe Giambrone, November 13, 2013[41]

In November of 2003, Senator Max Cleland resigned from the *9/11 Commission* investigation, directly disparaging it by way of the *Warren Commission* investigation. Senator Cleland said:

The *Warren Commission* blew it. I'm not going to be part of that. I'm not going to be part of looking at information only partially. I'm not going to be part of just coming to quick conclusions. I'm not going to be part of political pressure to do this or not do that (Boehlert).

The most obvious fact, to indicate that the true story of John F. Kennedy's slaying is not as the government has presented, is the cover-up itself. Elaborate cover-ups spanning 50 years cannot orchestrate themselves, and there must be compelling reasons for hiding the truth from the American people, or else it would simply be declassified and revealed. If the killing of the president was committed by a lone nut single shooter named Lee Harvey Oswald, because of his great love of Marxism, there would be no compelling reason to keep his files secret five decades after the fact. Quite the opposite, Mr. Oswald's clear guilt and personal history would

---

41 https://politicalfilm.wordpress.com/2013/11/13/jfk-cover-up-where-theres-smoke-theres-fire/

have been useful propaganda material in the ideological battle between the Western world and the Soviet bloc. The ongoing and arguably illegal suppression of assassination evidence by the US government should be taken as a clear indicator of some level of official complicity in the original assassination.

Despite the US government and major media pressing the official story for fifty years, still relatively few Americans believe it. By 2004, "74 percent" of Americans thought there was a "cover-up of the facts about the assassination of JFK" (Blanton). Today, polls show a majority firmly behind the conspiratorial view, with an April 2013 *Associated Press* finding that, "59 percent of Americans think multiple people were involved in a conspiracy."

Of course the 1979 *House Select Committee on Assassinations* (HSCA) determined the killing was "probably" a conspiracy, with a pathetic guess their final determination. Their committee was "unable to determine" the identities of other shooters or the "extent of the conspiracy" (Porter). This is more evidence of cover-up, especially so given the sheer number of documents to be released *after* 1979, and, even more damaging, those that remain secret to this day. We know of at least 1,100 multi-page records related to the JFK hit that remain classified.

Among those still classified records are details of the CIA's surveillance of Lee Harvey Oswald *prior* to the assassination (Morley, "Top 7..."). Characters kept shielded from public scrutiny include Bill Harvey who headed an assassination team for CIA code named "ZR-RIFLE." CIA operative David A. Phillips was allegedly seen with Oswald in Dallas in September of 1963, two months before the slaying of a president. At least 332 hidden pages concern E. Howard Hunt, a CIA thug and Nixon "plumber" (plugged leaks) involved in Watergate. Hunt would confess on his deathbed to being part of the JFK hit, as published in *Rolling Stone*, although specifics of his story may be inaccurate (Maier). In his confession E. Howard Hunt did name Cord Meyer, Bill Harvey, David Morales, David A. Phillips, Frank Sturgis and then Vice President Lyndon B. Johnson (Hedegaard).

E. Howard Hunt's "Death Bed Confession" has all the ingredients of an EZ dictate

The second JFK investigation, the 1979 HSCA, in no way got to the truth of the matter, and nowhere is this more clearly shown than in its failure to interview Jerrol Custer when it addressed whether the Kennedy X-rays were forgeries or not (HSCA, "Section IV"). Custer was the x-ray technician who took the pictures, and yet he was not brought in to clarify that the images were authentic. Custer testified in 1997 to the *Assassinations Records Review Board*: "When I looked into the skull – I remember seeing an apparatus in there... It was non-human. It had – I'm not sure if it was metallic or plastic..." His commanding officer, Dr. Ebersole returned late that night with additional skull fragments from Dallas. "High-ranking people had talked to [Ebersole]. And he suggested to me that everything I see from now on, I should forget" (ARRB, "Deposition..." p146).

Three days after Kennedy's killing, and just one day after Lee Harvey Oswald was also gunned down — while in police custody and having never confessed to anything — the assistant Attorney General of the United States, Nicholas Katzenbach, wrote a memo to a white house aide that included this point: "The public must be satisfied that Oswald was the assassin; that he did not have confederates who are still at large; and that the evidence was such that he would have been convicted at trial" (Katzenbach).

Clearly, at this early juncture there was no way for Nicholas Katzenbach to know these things as facts. In explaining his memo, Katzenbach told the *House Select Committee on Assassinations* that his emphasis was on full disclosure and not on pressing the lone assassin theory (HSCA, p.653). Katzenbach's premature memo also noted some conspiracy theories that the Soviets were behind the Kennedy killing or that the extreme right wing was behind it in order to blame it on leftists. "Unfortunately, the facts on Oswald seem about too pat, too obvious (Marxist, Cuba, Russian wife, etc.)" (Katzenbach).

So even as he relayed the (premature) determination of FBI agents that Oswald was responsible and that he acted alone, Katzenbach expressed a reservation that it seemed "too obvious" that Oswald was so blatantly linked to the Soviet bloc.

We see an official policy to stick to the lone assassin theory, and specifically not to blame the JFK hit on the Soviets or Cuba, from President Johnson as well. A phone call on November 29th, one week after the slaying, from the President to Senator Richard Russell, made clear his concern. Johnson said, "[W]e've got to take this out of the arena where they're testifying that Khrushchev and Castro did this and did that and kicking us into a war that can kill 40 million Americans in an hour..." The direct threat of nuclear war supposedly took precedence rather than full disclosure, at least from the mouth of President Johnson. This rationale for covering up some facts was already established and on the record, inside the white house, one week after President Kennedy's murder.

Discrepancies with the Oswald legend would emerge later. Particularly curious is this bit of skullduggery: "In one taped conversation, Oswald — or someone saying he was Oswald — called the Soviet embassy. Then-FBI Director J. Edgar Hoover listened to the tape and told President Lyndon Johnson that it wasn't Oswald's voice" (Rosenbaum). That tape disappeared forever. Perhaps Katzenbach's "too obvious" speculation was spot on.

Oliver Stone's JFK film included another spot on point. As *Associated Press* states plainly, "Pamphlets Oswald had in his possession bore an address of a local anti-Castro operation connected to a former FBI agent with ties to organized crime," (Porter). So was Lee Harvey Oswald supposed to be pro-Castro, anti-Castro, undercover or what?

A cognitive dissonance surrounds this issue, particularly in the corporate media. Investigators routinely report highly suspicious facts only to attempt to spin them away, to diminish their importance. An example of this behavior is former *Washington Post* reporter Jefferson Morley, who has taken on the Kennedy case. Claims Morley: "This is not about conspiracy, this is about transparency... I think the CIA should obey the law" (Porter).

The definition of conspiracy is when multiple parties, or an organization such as CIA, break the law. Establishment journalists are so terrified of accusing the government of conspiracy, that they even seem prepared to attack the English language rather than to open themselves up to accusations of being a dreaded "conspiracy theorist."

The CIA made its propaganda agenda clear in April of 1967 in a document entitled, *"Countering Critics of the Warren Report."* Therein, the agency sought to, "employ propaganda assets to answer and refute the attacks of the critics" (Nurnad). That meant "book reviews" and "feature articles" as well as "friendly elite contacts (especially politicians and editors)." Countering critics of the Warren Report with propaganda was a clear breach of the CIA's charter, and operating domestically was and remains illegal (FAS). That propaganda effort, similar to the more formal "Operation Mockingbird" (Louise), would constitute additional official conspiracies peripherally related to the killing of President John F. Kennedy. In other words, official cover-ups tend to veer into technically criminal activities.

Jefferson Morley, who already disparaged the idea of a JFK conspiracy earlier in the AP article, presented another curious revelation: "The idea that Lee Harvey Oswald was some unknown quantity to CIA officers was false... There was this incredible high-level attention to Oswald on the eve of the assassination."

On the eve of the assassination, says Morley, as in prior to the killing in Dallas by the alleged lone nut assassin who just decided out of the blue to murder a president passing by below his place of employment. There was not only attention to Oswald, it was "high-level attention," which was "incredible." Morley's evidence is hard to locate, as his sourcing was not included in that AP story.

Anti-Castro Cuban exiles, working with CIA, were monitoring Lee Harvey Oswald three months prior to the JFK assassination. A lawsuit was filed to release records connected with George Joannides, who was the, "chief of the CIA's anti-Castro 'psychological warfare' operations in Miami" (Morley). What makes Joannides even more relevant to the cover-up is that he served as the Central Intelligence Agency's "liason" to the HSCA in 1978-9, but he never revealed to the investigation his own involvement in 1963. George Joannides was, of course, an expert in psychological warfare, the art of disinformation — which is plentiful in this particular murder case. Joannides was later accused of obstructing justice by deceiving the congressional committee (Morley).

The fact that there has been a cover-up of the JFK assassination is undeniable. The conflicting conclusions of the two main investigations, Warren vs. HSCA, establish that a cover-up has taken place.

George Joannides

Ongoing suppression of evidence by CIA further establishes this cover-up. Defenders of the official story would attribute such illegal behavior to institutions avoiding embarrassment or hiding negligence. Establishment journalist Jefferson Morley is an example of this view, as his own conspiracy theory suggests that: "release would show the CIA trying to keep secret its own flawed performance before the assassination" (Porter).

Lee Harvey Oswald holds a Mannlicher-Carcano rifle and newspapers in a backyard

The majority of the American people don't see it that way, however. They believe a far more sinister explanation is more likely, and for good reasons. The CIA has a history of criminal activity including overthrowing democracies, torture and politically-motivated murders. The Kennedy killing would not have been an aberration in tactics, only in the choice of target.

Works Cited

Assassination Records Review Board, Assassination of John F. Kennedy, "Deposition of Jerrol Francis Custer," *Miller Reporting Company Inc.,* Washington DC, 28 Oct.1997, hosted at http://www.aarclibrary.org, *The Assassination Archives and Research Center,* Web, 10 Nov. 2013.

Associated Press (AP), "Belief In JFK Assassination Conspiracy Slipping, Poll Finds" The Associated Press, 3 Nov. 2013, hosted at huffingtonpost.com, The Huffington Post, Web, 10 Nov. 2013.

Blanton, Dana, "Poll: Most Believe 'Cover-Up' of JFK Assassination Facts," *Fox News*, foxnews.com, 18 June 2004, Web, 10 Nov. 2013.
Boehlert, Eric, "The president ought to be ashamed," *Salon*, Salon Media Group Inc., 21 Nov. 2003, Web. 10 Nov. 2013.

Federation of American Scientists (FAS), "The Evolution of the U.S. Intelligence Community-An

Historical Overview," *Page INTO22*, 23 Feb. 1996, Web, 10 Nov. 2013.

Hedegaard, Erik, "The Last Confessions of E. Howard Hunt," *Rolling Stone*, 5 April 2007, Web, Hosted at *The Wayback Machine*, archive.org, 11 Nov. 2013.

JFK. Dir. Oliver Stone. Warner Brothers, 1991. DVD.

Johnson, Lyndon B., "Telephone Conversation Between The President And Senator Russell," phone conversation, transcript, November 29, 1963, 8:55pm, p. 2, hosted at maryferrell.org, *Mary Ferrell Foundation*, Web, 10 Nov. 2013

Katzenbach, Nicholas, "Memorandum For Mr. Moyers," *FBI 62-109060 JFK HQ File, Section 18*, US Department of Justice, Federal Bureau of Investigation, 25 Nov. 1963, hosted at maryferrell.org, *The Mary Ferrell Foundation*, Web. 10 Nov. 2013.

Louise, Mary, " Operation Mockingbird: CIA Media Manipulation," The Reporters Committee for Freedom of the Press, Web, 11 Nov. 13.
Maier, Timothy W., "Deathbed confession: Who really killed JFK?" *Baltimore Post Examiner*, 2 July 2012, Web, 11 Nov. 2013.

Morley, Jeff, "Top 7 JFK files the CIA still keeps secret," *JFK Facts*, JFKFacts.org,10 Nov. 2013, Web, 10 Nov. 2013.

Morley, Jefferson, "Celebrated authors demand that the CIA come clean on JFK assassination," *Salon*, Salon Media Group Inc., 17 Dec. 2003, Web 10 Nov. 2013.

Nurnad, Clayton P., "Countering Critics of the Warren Report," *CIA no. 1035-960*, US Government, Central Intelligence Agency (CIA), reprinted in Stone, Oliver and Sklar, Zachary, "JFK: The Book of the Film (Applause Screenplay Series) First Edition," Applause Theatre & Cinema Books, 1 Feb.2000, p.550.

Porter, David, "5 decades later, some JFK probe files still sealed," *Associated Press*, Aug. 17, 2013, Web, 10 Nov. 2013.

Rosenbaum, Marcus D., "Inconsistencies Haunt Official Record of Kennedy's Death," *National Public Radio*, npr.org, 10 Nov. 2013, Web, 11 Nov. 2013.

Select Committee on Assassinations of the U.S. House of Representatives, *Report of the Select Committee on Assassinations of the U.S. House of Representatives*, Washington, DC: United States Government Printing Office, 1979, hosted at historymatters.com, History Matters, Web, 10 Nov. 2013.

Select Committee on Assassinations of the U.S. House of Representatives, "Volume VII, Section IV: Authenticity," Report of the Select Committee on Assassinations of the U.S. House of Representatives, *Washington, DC: United States Government Printing Office, 1979, hosted at John McAdams' Web Site,* Marquette University, *Web, 10 Nov. 2013.*

1.8 "Update on the man who killed police officer Tippit"

by Wim Dankbaar, September 18, 2012[42]

It is worth noting that Gary Marlow has lived until his death on April 4, 2007 in the knowledge that his picture (the one with Files in which he is wearing sunglasses) was on the website JFKmurdersolved.com, implicating him as the man who killed Tippit.

Marlow has never come forward to deny the allegation and/or expose Files as a liar. Probably because he was not identified by name. Files, nor his best friend Bruce Brychek, would never tell me his name, in spite of my pressure.

---

42 https://rechtiskrom.wordpress.com/2012/09/18/update-on-the-man-who-killed-police-officer-tippit/
    http://www.jfkmurdersolved.com/tip.htm

The man who killed J.D. Tippit according to James Files has since been identified as Gary Eugene Marlow. Gary Marlow was a lifetime friend of James Files since school time. He died in 2007 from cancer.

I recall a telephone conversation with Bruce in 2006, in which I explained that it would really help the credibility of James Files to disclose the identity of the man he implicates as the Tippit killer. Bruce responded that the man had recently been contacted – he did not specify how or by whom – with exactly that request, but the man had indicated that under no circumstance his name should be revealed, not even after his death. "I don't need this shit" Bruce quoted him, "not now or later, I don't want it for my family".

To me this whole order of events adds greatly to the credibility of James Files. Why the heck would he implicate a long life friend in the events on November 22, 1963 in Dallas? While that man is still alive and could come forward any time to deny the accusation and expose Files as a liar?

This is a risk that no hoax with common sense would take. Instead, we now know that Marlow was aware of it, but never chose to come forward to deny it. In fact, he has confirmed it. Of course, a denial would never have stood a chance as he could never deny he is indeed the man with sunglasses in the picture with Files. Nor could he deny that he was a friend of Files. Shit would have hit the fan if he had come forward. As a free man, unlike Files, he stood much to lose. So he remained silent, wanting to take his secret to his grave. It is not thanks to him that his secret emerged from his grave.

Bruce Brychek, best living friend of James Files, posted the message below on my forum on April 27, 2007. This was before I knew that the man was Gary Marlow and had indeed died. I learned that in October of 2008 when I was approached by Janet Schroder, whose sister had dated James Files and later had married his friend Gary Marlow. She had come across my website and recognized Gary Marlow. So Files has never disclosed the name himself, true to his promise.

Janet emailed me several pictures of Gary Marlow. Like the one above. This is a fragment of a picture of Gary Marlow's wedding with Janet's sister in 1966. For privacy reasons I cut out Janet and her bride sister. So it only shows Gary Marlow and James Files, who was his best man at the wedding.

1.9 "Dallas Patrolman J.D. Tippit's shooter recently dies"
by Bruce Patrick Brychek, April 27, 2007

Dear Mr. Wim Dankbaar, and Fellow JFK Forum Members,

FOR THE RECORD:

Dallas Patrolman J. D. Tippit's shooter has recently died.

Tippit was not killed by Lee Harvey Oswald as was/is claimed by the U.S. Government, the U.S. News Media, and last but not least, The Warren Commission Report.

The shooter was in route to meet, and kill Lee Harvey Oswald at the Texas Theatre where Oswald had been directed to go by his CIA handler,

David Atlee Phillips, who was also James E. Sutton's CIA handler.

David Atlee Phillips, Sam Giancana, and Charles Nicoletti all probably had some knowledge, which cannot be quantified at this point in time.

At his request, prior to his death, to protect his wife, and family, he has requested that his name never be released.

Respectfully,

Bruce Patrick Brychek.

TIMELINE 1 (by Janet Schoder)

1938- J.D. (John Dee) Marlow born in Alabama 10/17/38

1940- Gary Eugene Marlow born in Bessemer, Alabama 10/23/40.

1941- Joan Marlow (Kehring) born in Chicago, Il. March 1st, 1941.

1942- James Earl Files born in Oakman, Alabama January 24, 1942.

1943- Eleanor Files(Schramm) born April 12, 1943 Janet Schoder (Kehring) born Oct.. 27, 1943.

1957 - about- Gary Marlow & James Files graduated elementary school on 18th & Lake St. in Melrose Park, Illinois. Faith Johnson went to

Proviso East High School in Maywood, IL. Jim dropped out in freshman year. Gary Marlow dropped out of High School too. Not sure what high school. Probably Proviso also.

1958- Faith dated Gary Marlow for short time then later married J.D. Marlow (John Dee), Gary's brother. Jim dated Eleanor Schramm and took her to a Prom arranged by both their mothers.

1959 - James Files joined military and sent to Laos.

1960 - Sept.? James Files discharged from military. Joan Kehring and family move from N. Second Ave. in Maywood, Ill. to 34th Ave. in Melrose Park, Ill. in June 1960.

1961 - James Files dated Eleanor Schramm early in 1961. She was friends with Joan & Janet Kehring & walked home from Proviso with Janet a lot. She was a junior at Proviso East in Maywood. Broke up because her family didn't approve of him.

1962- Joan Kehring started dating James Files on 11/5/62. Met him at gas station on Lake St. & Mannheim Rd., Melrose Park(Stone Park?) Janet Kehring home on leave for Christmas from Air Force and met Jim Files.. Joan saw him on Christmas Day.

1963- April 12th. Easter. James Files broke up with Joan Kehring after giving her big box of candy. Joan started dating Albert-Al-Helton that worked with Jim at the gas station.

1963-   Summer-Joan saw Eleanor at gas station on Mannheim & she showed her her engagement ring to James Files. 10/2/63 or 10/5/63 Jim & Eleanor married in church on 5th Av. near Lake St. in Maywood, Il.

1963- John F. Kennedy assassinated in Dallas on 11/22/63. James Files claimed to be the Grassy Knoll shooter & Gary Marlow was the shooter of J.D. Tippit.

1964-   Jan.17th. Jim & Eleanor Files moved into new apartment on 34th Av. in Melrose Park across street from Joan Kehring's parents house. About Friday, July 31, Eleanor badly injured in car accident in Indiana on way home from moving Jim's folks back to Kentucky. Aug.7th-Joan helped Jim pack to move out of apartment across street.

1964- Sometime in Spring. Jim & Eleanor over in Joan's parents driveway on 34th Av. in Melrose Park & introduced her to Gary Eugene Marlow. They dated for about 2 months then he had to leave to go help his mother in Fl. so he said.

1965-   June 21st. Gary asked Joan out again after he came back to Melrose Park and they started dating again. He was gone about one year.

1966- Joan Kehring married Gary Marlow with James Files as his best man & Joan's sister Janet as maid of honor at little white church in Melrose Park on 37th & Division. Gary's brother J.D. Marlow, wife Faith and two daughters, Kerry & Cindy there and at reception in Kehring's side yard at 1544 N. 34th Ave. in Melrose Park. Also, Gary and J.D.'s parents were there.

1966-   Sept. 26- Kathy Files born to Jim & Eleanor Files.

1967, 1968, 1969- Joan & Gary Marlow close friends with Jim & Eleanor. J.D. & Faith Marlow saw them too.

1968-   About April- J.D. told Gary Faith wanted him to leave. Having marital problems. April 20 Jim & Eleanor were in the wedding party for Eleanor's brother Ed & Julie Schramm. Joan & Gary went to the reception.

1969-   Jim Files & Faith Marlow seeing each other a lot. J.D. & Faith and Jim & Eleanor broke up. After J.D. lived with Jim Files in an apartment for a while, he lived with Joan & Gary. About 1970,1971 ? he moved back to Alabama.

1972-   J.D. Marlow killed in car accident in Alabama on Oct. 31-Halloween. Gary Marlow accused Jim of having something to do with his brother's death and broke off their friendship.

1981-   Joan and Gary Marlow divorced after Gary met Mary over at Ed & Julie Schramm's house, Eleanor's brother.

1982-   Gary Marlow and Mary married.

2007-   Gary Marlow died in Conyers, Georgia on April 2, 2007.

2008-   Jan. 25th, 2008 Janet came across Wim Dankbaar's website "JFKmurdersolved.com" and saw book "Files on JFK" and found out about James Files claim he was the "Grassy Knoll" gunman. Shocked!!!!!!!!!! Told sister Joan Marlow in Fl. Eleanor (Schramm, Files) Albert died Dec. 19, 2008. Joan & Janet started writing Jim Files in Stateville Prison, Joliet, Il. Janet in Oct. and Joan in Dec.

1.10 Cuban Intelligence Was in Contact With Oswald

by Sarah Pruitt, October 27, 2017

Here are the 10 most revealing highlights from the 2,800 newly declassified JFK assassination files.

On October 26, the National Archives made public more than 2,800 files relating to the 1963 assassination of President John F. Kennedy, just hours before the deadline set for their final release by Congress in the 1992 JFK Records Collection Act.

President Donald Trump announced he was blocking the immediate release of some 300 files, citing concerns from U.S. intelligence and national security agencies. Pending a six-month review, the archives will release the final batch of files, with redactions, on a rolling basis.

Despite the last-minute action by President Trump, the release of thousands of JFK-related documents is more than enough to keep historians, journalists, assassination experts and conspiracy theorists occupied for a long time to come. From the massive array of handwritten notes, memos, interview transcripts and intelligence reports—many of them partly or entirely illegible—a few intriguing and surprising revelations have emerged so far:

Evidence From the JFK Assassination Case

1) The KGB believed there was a well-organized conspiracy behind JFK's assassination—possibly involving LBJ In December 1966, FBI Director J. Edgar Hoover forwarded a memo to the White House that described the reaction of Soviet and Communist Party officials to Kennedy's assassination. The memo stated that according to the FBI's source, Communist officials believed there was a well-organized "ultra-right" conspiracy behind the assassination.

Not only that, but: "Our source added that in the instructions from Moscow, it was indicated that...the KGB was in possession of data purporting to indicate President Johnson was responsible for the assassination." For good measure, the Soviets claimed no connection with Oswald, who they considered a "neurotic maniac who was disloyal to his own country and everything else."

2) But—Oswald was overheard speaking to a KGB official just two months before the assassination. On September 28, 1963, the CIA intercepted a call Oswald made to the Russian embassy in Mexico City. On the call, he can be heard speaking in "broken Russian" to Consul Valeriy Vladimirovich Kostikova, an "identified KGB officer," according to the document.

3) An alleged Cuban intelligence officer knew Oswald, and praised his shooting abilities. The transcript of a 1967 cablegram recounted how a man named Angel Ronaldo Luis Salazar was interrogated at the Cuban embassy in Mexico

City the year before by Ramiro Jesus Abreu Quintana, "an identified Cuban intelligence officer," about Kennedy's assassination. During the interrogation, Salazar claimed he remarked that Oswald must have been a good shot. According to him, Abreu replied "Oh, he was quite good….I knew him."

4) Someone phoned in a death threat on Oswald to the FBI the day before he was murdered. In a document dated November 24, 1963, J. Edgar Hoover weighed in impassively on Jack Ruby's fatal shooting of Oswald that day, stating: "There is nothing further on the Oswald case except that he is dead." Hoover also recounted a call received by the FBI's Dallas office from a man saying he was part of a committee formed to kill Oswald. According to Hoover, the FBI urged the Dallas police to protect JFK's assassin, but Ruby was nonetheless able to fire the fatal shots.

5) The U.S. government debated hiring gangsters to kill Fidel Castro, or paying Cuban assassins to do so. At least two of the documents outline some of the Kennedy administration's policy and actions toward Cuban dictator Fidel Castro. According to a 1975 document simply titled "CASTRO," the CIA was involved in assassination plots against Castro as early as late 1959 and early 1960, even during preparations for the Bay of Pigs. In 1962, a proposal was put forward called "Operation Bounty," which would create "a system of financial rewards...for killing or delivering alive known Communists."

As part of the operation, leaflets were to be distributed via air to Cuba, including one announcing "a .02¢ reward for the delivery of Castro." The low amount was restricted to Castro himself, and was reportedly meant to "denigrate" the Cuban leader. Another potential plan, according to another 1975 report, involved getting poison botulism pills to "organized crime figures," who would then pass them to their Cuban contacts in the hopes of reaching someone close to Castro. The same document also includes an FBI memo stating that Robert Kennedy told the agency that the CIA had hired an intermediary to approach Mafia boss Sam Giancana offering to pay him to hire someone to kill Castro.

6) A mysterious man known as "El Mexicano" (believed to be a Cuban rebel army captain) may have accompanied Oswald in Mexico City. A CIA document containing handwritten notes indicated Oswald may have been accompanied in Mexico by a man dubbed "El Mexicano," who is believed to have been a Cuban rebel army captain who later defected to the United States. Identified by another source as Francisco Rodriguez Tamayo, he was said in another newly released document to be the head of an anti-Castro training camp in Louisiana.

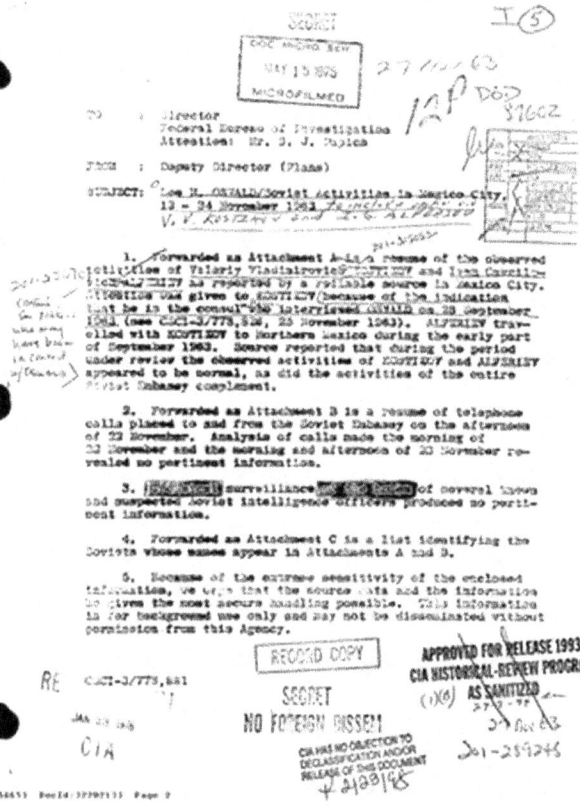

A handout image of a FBI report about Lee Harvey Oswald in Mexico City released by the National Archives as part of nearly 3,000 previously sealed or redacted documents related to the 1963 assassination of US President John F. Kennedy.[43]

---

43 (Credit: National Archives Handout/EPA-EFE/REX/Shutterstock)

7) LBJ used to go around saying JFK's murder was payback for the U.S. killing of a Vietnamese president. In an April 1975 deposition at CIA headquarters in Langley, Virginia, Richard Helms (director of CIA under both Lyndon Johnson and Richard Nixon) testified that Johnson claimed JFK was killed in retribution for the assassination of Ngo Dinh Diem, who was killed as part of a U.S.-backed coup earlier in 1963. "He certainly used to say that in the early days of his Presidency," Helms testified, "and where he got that idea I don't know."

8) The FBI warned Robert Kennedy about a book detailing his affair with Marilyn Monroe. In July 1964, the FBI warned then-Attorney General Robert Kennedy, JFK's younger brother, about a soon-to-be-published book that included juicy details about Kennedy's intimate relationship with Marilyn Monroe. The book's author, Robert A. Capell, claimed that when Monroe threatened to expose the relationship, Kennedy may have had something to do with her death. "It should be noted," the document states, "that the allegation concerning the Attorney General and Miss Monroe has been circulated in the past and has been branded as utterly false."

9) Someone tipped off a London reporter about "big news" in the United States 25 minutes before Kennedy was shot. In a memo dated November 26, 1963, FBI Deputy Director James Angleton recorded that British Security Service (MI5) had reported a call made to the Cambridge

News on the evening of November 22. The caller told the paper's senior reporter to "call the American Embassy in London for some big news," before hanging up. By MI5's calculations, Kennedy was shot in Dallas 25 minutes after the call came in.

10) A week or so before the assassination, a man in a New Orleans bar bet $100 that President Kennedy would be dead within three weeks. In the days after Kennedy was shot, the Secret Service recorded notes from an interview with a man named Robert Rawls, who was at the time a patient at the U.S. Naval Hospital in Charleston, South Carolina.

A November 22, 1963 photograph of Jackie Kennedy and Secret Service agent Clint Hill climbing on the back of the limousine after U.S. President John F. Kennedy was shot, juxtaposed with the current scene in Dallas. (Credit: Houston Chronicle, Cody Duty/AP Photo)

According to what Rawls told an officer of the Naval Intelligence Unit, he'd been in a bar in New Orleans, Louisiana 10 days to two weeks earlier, when he overheard a man try to bet $100 on Kennedy's imminent demise. Rawls, who admitted being half in the bag himself, didn't catch the man's name, and didn't even remember the name of the bar. At the time, he thought the bet was "drunk talk," and laughed it off.

Ex-CIA Officer Weighs in on the JFK Files

Former CIA officer and author Robert Baer, who led the investigation in History's "JFK Declassified: Tracking Oswald" program, believes the biggest revelation to come out of the newest file release is that the White House and intelligence agencies are continuing to conceal all that was known about Lee Harvey Oswald before the assassination, and how much information was withheld from the official investigation into the events of November 22, 1963. "They've had 25 years to redact and protect sources and methods," Baer says. "What they're covering up...is the actual cover-up on Oswald, and there was one. I have seen no evidence that there's any sort of government conspiracy, but the cover-up—withholding from the Warren Commission, destroying documentation—it's just there. It's undisputed."

Baer hasn't had a chance to review all the newly released documents, but he believes many of the most important documents, and eyewitnesses, related to Oswald's plot to kill Kennedy will never be made public. These include information about Oswald's known connections with Cuban exiles in Dallas, who may have known of his assassination plans and sent word back to Havana, as well as interviews with a key eyewitness at the Cuban consulate, where Oswald reportedly bragged openly about his plans to kill the U.S. president.

If the full trove of government records related to JFK's assassination were ever to be made public, Baer has an idea of what they would show. "I think what happened, without seeing all the documents, is that the assassination could have been stopped," Baer says. "The Secret Service should have been informed, Oswald should have been confronted before Kennedy's visit...It could have been stopped." He believes "once the government understood this [was preventable], they closed down the investigation."

"It's not what the conspiracy theorists think—the guy with the black umbrella, the shooter on the grassy knoll," Baer says. "The crime is the cover-up."

1.11. Other Special Guests

By Popeye[44]

Ed Lansdale was a CIA agent whose cover title was that of an Air Force Colonel and later General, who worked directly for CIA Director Allen Dulles. Lansdale specialized in political-psychological warfare operations, and manipulation of governments. The photo of him in Dealey Plaza on November 22nd 1963 reveals a deep level of involvement with certain factions within the CIA in the planning, operational phase, cover story, and cover up of the assassination of President John F. Kennedy in Dallas on November 22nd 1963. Such operations (Coup d'état) were Gen. Lansdale's specialty.

George H.W. Bush was working for the CIA at least as early as 1961; more than likely he was recruited in his college days, at Yale, when he was in the Skull and Bones Society. He and his wife Barbara moved to Houston where he ran an offshore oil drilling business, Zapata Offshore Co., which was a CIA front company with rigs located all over the world, making it very convenient for him to vanish for weeks at a time

---

44 http://www.federaljack.com/why-was-cia-coup-detat-expert-ed-lansdale-in-dealey-plaza-when-jfk-was-shot/
Too bad EZ killed this website

on CIA business where one would suspect what he was doing.

Bush was a major organizer and recruiter for the Bay of Pigs invasion, which was codenamed Operation ZAPATA. Col. Fletcher Prouty, former Pentagon high ranking official, who was the basis for the "Col. X" character in Oliver Stone's "JFK", obtained two Navy ships for the operation that were repainted to non-Navy colors and then renamed HOUSTON and BARBARA.

Many photographers caught GWHB on their films. Most of these have been recently (since Bush published the memoirs of an imaginary personality) evaporated from the internet. The only surviving site in the US is yola.[45] It is worth reading all of it. Here, I only show the site's content related to CIA GWHB's role.

---

45 http://jfkrevelations.yolasite.com/

George H.W. "Poppy" Bush is one of the few who could never recall where he was or what he was doing when JFK was assassinated; as a matter of fact, for over 20 years, he could not recall any details at all. He was 39 years old at the time and chairman of the Harris County (Houston) Republican Party and an outspoken critic of JFK. But on 21 November 1963, GHWB was staying at the Sheraton Hotel in downtown Dallas and spoke that very evening to the American Association of Oil Drilling Contractors. Sometime later, he was reportedly at "the ratification meeting" at the home of Clint Murchison, Sr., receiving last minute instructions and toasting JFK's murder the night before it happened. [NOTE: Madeleine Duncan Brown has written about this event in her book, Texas in the Morning (1997). It was corroborated by Nigel Turner in Part 9, "The Guilty Men", of "The Men who Killed Kennedy"...]

Finally, I do not wish to withhold from you the photos taken by employees of CIA's photo-forgery laboratory.

The same men have been seen visiting the Soviet embassy in Mexico City, the same time Lee Harvey Oswald was in Mexico.[46]

---

46 It provided the lousy (for that time impressive) photocomposition presented by the Life Journal cover (shown in section 1.7 in this book): Oswald's head pasted over an unknown man's body who was obviously not holding a long heavy rifle with his left hand.

CHAPTER 2
Robert Francis (Bobby) Kennedy

Young-looking faces: Robert Kennedy friendly chatting with César Chávez

"If they're going to shoot, they'll shoot."

This quote of Bobby's was reported by his aide and confidential friend Fred Dutton, April 11, 1968.[47]

Robert F. Kennedy, who had made many enemies during his time on the Washington scene, was well aware of the dangers he faced in trying to reclaim the Presidency lost in 1963 when his brother was killed in Dallas. Fate befell him just after midnight on June 5, 1968, moments after declaring victory in the California Democratic primary. Escorted through a kitchen pantry in the Ambassador Hotel, RFK was assailed by Palestinian Sirhan Sirhan firing a .22 pistol. Kennedy was shot multiple times, and five others were wounded by gunfire. While bodyguards and others wrestled with Sirhan, who continued to shoot wildly, Kennedy collapsed in a pool of blood. He died the following day. In the assassinations of President Kennedy and Martin Luther King, Jr., the evidence tying the alleged assassins to the case was circumstantial and almost too neat. But here, Sirhan was apprehended on the scene firing a gun within a couple of feet of Kennedy. An open-and-shut case? Ironically, the RFK assassination has the starkest physical and eyewitness evidence indicating a conspiracy involving Sirhan and at least one additional gunman.

---

47 https://www.maryferrell.org/pages/Robert_Kennedy_
    Assassination.html

Sirhan Bishara Sirhan

2.1 Who was Sirhan Sirhan?

An early indication that there might be more than meets the eye in this case came with the discovery of Sirhan's diaries. Page after page featured repetitive writing, with such phrases as "RFK must die" and "Robert F. Kennedy must be assassinated" occurring over and over, coupled with such curious phrases as "pay to the order of" and "my determination to eliminate RFK is becoming more the [sic] more of an unshakable obsession." An entry from May 18 noted that

"Robert F. Kennedy must be assassinated before 5 June 68."

Sirhan Bishara Sirhan was born in Jerusalem in 1944, and moved with his family to the U.S. when he was 12. He had been employed exercising horses at the Santa Anita racetrack until an accident in 1966. He was obsessed with mystical powers, apparently believing that he was learning to control events with his mind, and fascinated with hypnosis. Psychiatrists determined that he was highly susceptible to hypnosis, and may have produced his strange writings while in a trance.

Sirhan has continually maintained that he has no memory of writing in his notebook, nor of the events that night at the Ambassador Hotel. This has led many to believe that he may have been a real "Manchurian Candidate," programmed to shoot RFK and then fail to recall who put him up to it.

2.2. The Polka-Dotted Dress Girl

Sirhan was seen in the hotel —including in the pantry itself— in the company of a girl wearing a polka-dotted dress. The girl and another male companion were seen running from the pantry after the shooting. RFK campaign worker Sandy Serrano, taking a break out on a balcony, saw them run from the hotel, the woman gleefully shouting "We shot him. We shot him." When

Serrano asked who they meant, the girl replied "Senator Kennedy."

Unbelievable as this sounds, their behavior was corroborated by LAPD officer Paul Sharaga, who was told the same thing by an elderly couple in the parking lot behind the hotel. Sharaga was the source of an All Points Bulletin (APB) on the suspects. The girl was described consistently by most of the witnesses: dirty blond hair, well-built, with a crooked or "funny" nose, wearing a white dress with blue or black polka-dots.

There were many other witnesses to the polka-dotted dress girl, in the hotel and in the company of Sirhan in the weeks prior to the assassination.

2.3 A Second Gun

There was other eyewitness testimony of a second shooter. Dr. Marcus McBoom saw a man with a partially-concealed pistol in his hand, running from the pantry. Don Schulman reported seeing a security guard at Kennedy's side pull out his gun during the attack.

These accounts and others take on added significance in light of the Robert Kennedy's autopsy report. Coroner Thomas Naguchi determined that RFK had been shot three times, all from the rear at a steep upward angle, with powder burns indicating that the fatal shot was fired at point blank range, 1 or 2 inches away. But

no witness put Sirhan near enough, or behind
Kennedy; eyewitness accounts consistently
placed him firing at RFK from the front, and not
closer than a few feet away.

Sirhan's Iverson .22 revolver held a maximum
of 8 bullets. Two bullets were removed from RFK,
and five from other victims. One of the three
bullets to strike RFK grazed him and was
determined by LAPD to have gone into the ceiling,
though it was never recovered. That accounts for
all 8, even conceding the LAPD's reconstruction
which explained away bullet holes found in ceiling
tiles, by positing that one of the bullets had
ricocheted back down and struck victims (causing
two ceiling holes in the process).

What is not accounted for are bullet holes in
the doorframe where RFK's party had entered
the pantry. Photographs taken by the FBI, LAPD,
and AP show apparent bullet holes, which have
been circled and initialed. Some pictures show
police officers depicted in the photos told author
Vincent Bugliosi that they had observed an actual
bullet embedded in the wood of the center door
frame.

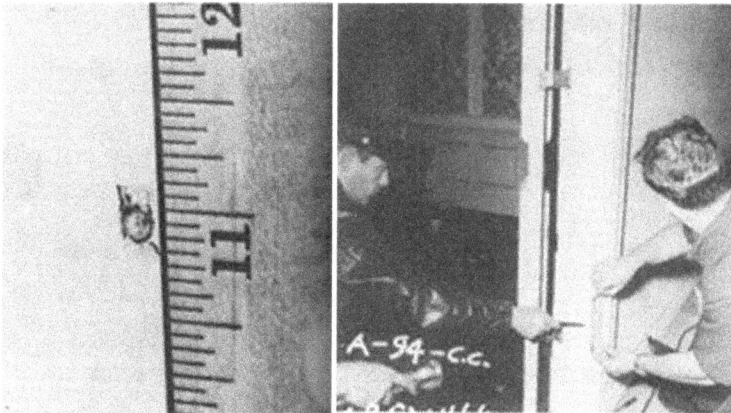

Left Panel: Size of bullet hole. Right Panel: LAPD officers measuring apparent bullet holes in pantry doorframe

Hotel waiter Martin Patrusky said that police officers told him that they had dug two bullets out of the center divider. FBI agent William Bailey, in the pantry within hours of the shooting, said he could see the base of the bullet in the center divider pointing at them; one AP photo is labeled "Bullet found near Kennedy shooting scene."

Other confirmation comes from photographers and even the carpenter who assisted in removal of the door frame for police evidence.

In 2004, a tape recording which featured the gunfire in the pantry surfaced. Made by Polish freelance journalist Stanislaw Pruszynski, the tape was analyzed by a team led by Philip Van Praag, who announced that the tape revealed thirteen shots fired in the space of five seconds.

Sirhan's gun held eight bullets. As in the JFK acoustics evidence, this finding is the subject of debate.

2.4 Special Unit Senator

What did the LAPD do with all this evidence of conspiracy, and more not mentioned here? The files of their investigation, released twenty years after the assassination, show that the evidence was ignored, and in some cases actively countered. The LAPD set up a Special Unit Senator (SUS) group to handle the investigation, and the tactics of some of its members have been called into question. Enrique Hernandez, who conducted polygraph exams for SUS, was among the most aggressive.

Sandy Serrano, one of the prime witnesses to the girl in the polka-dotted dress and a male companion, was browbeaten by Hernandez into retracting her story. The following exchange is typical of the treatment given Serrano in lengthy interview sessions:

Hernandez: "I think you owe it to Senator Kennedy, the late Senator Kennedy, to come forth, to be a woman about this. If he, and you don't know and I don't know whether he's a witness right now in this room watching what we're doing in here. Don't shame his death by keeping this thing up. I have compassion for you.

I want to know why. I want to know why you did what you did. This is a very serious thing."

Serrano: "I seen those people!"

Hernandez: "No, no, no, no, Sandy. Remember what I told you about that: you can't say you saw something when you didn't see it..."

Eventually Serrano went along with the LAPD. And once she had retracted her story, the "fact" that Serrano had made up the story was apparently used to discredit other corroborating witnesses, who generally didn't know that their story was being repeated by others. The pattern of isolation and even intimidation recurs repeatedly in the transcripts and tapes of interviews, many of whom retracted statements under pressure. In other cases, the interviews in the record do not contain information that the witness has later stated he or she told the police, and it is not always clear where the truth lies. Some evidence was simply ignored — or lost. This missing evidence included the memo of Paul Sharaga, the officer who interviewed the elderly couple who also saw a woman and man fleeing the scene of the shooting gleefully shouting "We shot him! We shot him!" Sharaga had enough presence of mind to retain the original mimeograph.

The door frames, which according to trained law enforcement officers had bullets embedded in them, were destroyed by the LAPD after Sirhan's trial. They were not admitted into evidence in that trial. Other evidence, including photographs taken in the pantry by a teenager named Scott Enyart, never saw the light of day.

The LAPD Summary Report deals with many of the witnesses to accomplices or other evidence indicating conspiracy, and dismisses them all in a variety of ways. In some cases, for example polka-dotted dress girl witness Booker Griffin, witnesses are said to have admitted making up their story, but inspection of the raw LAPD files fail to show such retractions.

2.5 The Trial of Sirhan Sirhan

But what about Sirhan's defense team? Wouldn't this evidence have to be given to his lawyers, and then come out a trial? Several factors worked against this. First, not all evidence was shared with Sirhan's lawyers. Even the autopsy report, whose conclusion of point-blank shots from the rear would seemingly exonerate Sirhan of RFK's actual murder, was not given to the defense until they had already stipulated Sirhan's guilt. The defense early on decide to pursue a "diminished capacity" defense, and the autopsy report didn't change that strategy.

Late Lawrence Teeter, attorney for Sirhan Sirhan

It is important to understand the motivations of each side in the legal system's "great engine of truth." Neither side had anything to gain by bringing in evidence of conspiracy. For the prosecution, it would simply muddle what otherwise seemed a simple case. And for the defense, conspiracy implies pre-meditation, and thus knowing guilt. Introducing evidence of accomplices would not be helpful to their client.

Sirhan Sirhan was his own worst enemy at the trial, using it as a platform for expressing anti-Semitic political views and touting the Arab cause. Whether these issues were really motivation for a shooting he claims not to remember executing remains a mystery. Finally, Sirhan's later attorney Lawrence Teeter uncovered evidence that Sirhan's lead trial lawyer, Grant Cooper, was compromised. Cooper was on one of the defense teams in the Friar's

Club scandal case; one of the defendants in that case was none other than Johnny Roselli, who had been a prime participant in the so-called "CIA-Mafia plots" to assassinate Fidel Castro. One day grand jury papers were found on Cooper's desk at counsel table, possibly planted there, perhaps by Roselli himself. Cooper faced a potential indictment over this incident, which could be grounds for disbarment, and the matter was left pending for the duration of the Sirhan trial. Afterwards, Cooper was let off with a $1000 fine.

Sirhan Bishara Sirhan was found guilty of first-degree murder and sentenced to death. While he was on death row, California abolished the death penalty, and commuted his sentence to life in prison, where he remains. Attorney Lawrence Teeter was fighting for a retrial at the time of his own death in 2005.

2.6 Ballistics Reviews

Ted Charach produced a documentary entitled "The Second Gun" in 1970, and questions continued to grow around the RFK case in the early 1970s. Criminalistics professor Herbert MacDonnell had signed an affidavit in 1973 stating that a bullet removed from RFK's neck, exhibit #47, could not have been fired from Sirhan's gun. He further stated that, based on the differing number of cannelures (grooves), it could not have been fired from the same gun as exhibit #54, a bullet removed from victim William Weisel. In a 1974 public hearing, California state crime lab veteran Lowell Bradford concurred.

Paul Schrade and Allard Lowenstein:
both pursued the RFK case for many years

In 1975, a court-appointed panel of seven ballistics experts was convened. While the headlines coming from the panel's work read "RFK Second Gun Theory Ruled Out," the reality was more subtle. Lowell Bradford, one of the panel members, said the question of a second gunman was "more open than before."

Subsequent research has uncovered serious problems with the marking of evidence bullets. Following the trail of Pasadena criminalist William Harper, researcher Rose Lynn Mangan discovered evidence of a "switch" of crime scene bullets. For example, she found that the Kennedy neck bullet (#47), which should have a "TN31" etched in its base, instead says "DWTN." There is reason to believe that even the Sirhan gun was swapped with another gun. LAPD criminologist DeWayne Wolfer had in fact introduced into evidence at Sirhan's trial the test gun, and represented it as the murder weapon, despite the different serial numbers.

It is worth noting that the 1975 panel discovered that two bullets allegedly removed from Sirhan's car contained traces of wood on both the base and the tip. Were these bullets dug out of the door frame?

Stalking RFK?

Such malfeasance on the part of the LAPD may be hard to believe. But the dismissive treatment of witnesses to Sirhan's accomplices is hard to refute, despite attempts to do so.

There were pre-assassination sightings of Sirhan in the company of a woman whose description matches the polka-dotted dress girl, and these sightings indicate that they were stalking Robert Kennedy.

On May 20, night manager Albert LaBeau of Robbie's Restaurant in Pomona encountered a man with a coat thrown over his arm - in the company of young woman. The pair were aggressively trying to gain access to a lunchroom where RFK would be - climbing over a stair railing in one of multiple attempts. LaBeau picked Sirhan's photo out of a set of 25 pictures of young dark-skinned males. Ten days later, a campaign worker named Laverne Botting was approached by a young woman and two men, trying to get a copy of Robert Kennedy's schedule. Her story was corroborated by another volunteer, Ethel Crehan.

Portion of Sirhan's May 18 diary entry

On June 1, three days before the primary, Dean Pack was hiking with his son in the Santa Ana mountains when they came upon a young man who resembled Sirhan, shooting a pistol in the company of a girl and another man. The three were quite hostile; Pack had a "funny sensation

that it would be possible for them to put a bullet
in your back."

Several witnesses saw a similar-looking girl, in
a polka-dotted dress, in the Ambassador Hotel on
the night of the primary. Irene Gizzi saw three
people, matching the trio seen by others, and
noted that they didn't seem to fit in with the
exuberant crowd. As noted before, the girl and
another man were seen in the pantry, rushing out
of it, and leaving the hotel gleefully shouting "We
shot him!"

2.7 The "Walking Bible"

Another strange story in the RFK case
concerns Jerry Owen, the "Walking Bible." Owen
himself went to authorities shortly after the
assassination, with the story that he had
happened to give Sirhan and another man a lift,
and had subsequently gone to the Ambassador
Hotel to collect $300 for a horse he was going to
sell to Sirhan. Owen said he encountered there a
blonde girl and two other men.

In the end, the LAPD determined that Owen,
whose background of criminal violations included
a conviction for arson in conjunction with a
church building, was telling a tale. But why would
he make up such a story?

Authors Bill Turner and Jonn Christian
researched the Owen story and interviewed Bill

Powers, a cowboy who ran Wild Bill's Stables less than a mile from where Owen lived. Powers told them that Owen had told him, before the assassination, about a horse trainer named Sirhan. Powers also said that had seen Sirhan in the back seat of Owen's car during a visit where Owen flashed large bills to pay off a pickup truck Powers had sold him.

If Owen knew Sirhan, was his story a pre-emptive cover story for meeting up at the Ambassador Hotel, possibly to supply a getaway vehicle?

2.8 No Parole

Sirhan is still serving out a life sentence in a California prison. Following the 9/11 attacks, he was for years held in solitary confinement. On occasions when he is up for parole, his case is always denied for lack of remorse (Sirhan claims no memory of the crime).

His 2016 parole hearing was unique, in that 91-year-old RFK aide and pantry shooting victim Paul Schrade attended. Schrade, who was behind RFK, believes that Sirhan shot him, but did not shoot Kennedy. At the hearing, he apologized to Sirhan, saying "I should have been here long ago and that's why I feel guilty for not being here to help you and to help me."

Schrade spoke at the hearing about the case for a second gunman. When the commissioner at one point interjected "Quite frankly, you're losing us," Schrade shot back "I think you've been lost for a long time."

Schrade has been joined in 2018 in his belief that RFK's murder remains unsolved by no less than Robert Kennedy Jr., Kennedy's son, as reported in the Washington Post.

2.9 Who Killed RFK?

Sirhan Sirhan was in the pantry firing a gun that night at Robert Kennedy, with intent to kill. But the autopsy report, coupled with dozens of eyewitnesses to the scene, cast grave doubt on the otherwise obvious conclusion that Sirhan actually fired the shots that hit RFK. Furthermore, the evidence is strong that Sirhan was stalking Kennedy in the company of a young blond girl and another male companion.

Many researchers have cast suspicion on Thane Eugene Cesar, a security guard with right-wing views on race who was escorting Kennedy by the arm through the pantry. Cesar was seen drawing his gun and possibly firing it, and told false stories about a .22 he owned (that he had sold it before the assassination, rather than after). But at least one witness claimed to see a different gunman to the rear of Kennedy firing the fatal shots.

The girl in the polka-dotted dress was never found — the LAPD insisted that campaign worker Valerie Schulte was the girl seen by some, despite differences in her appearance and clothing. There was another man, Michael Wayne, who was seen running from the pantry and subsequently tackled and taken away for questioning. Wayne had similarity in appearance to one of the individuals reported to have been seen in the company of Sirhan, and more intriguingly he had in his possession the business card of radical Minuteman Keith Duane Gilbert.

Sirhan may be lying when he claims to have no memory of the assassination. Journalist Robert Kaiser, who worked with Sirhan extensively as part of the defense team, caught him in several lies and presents in his book "R.F.K. Must Die!" a nuanced treatment of Sirhan as having multiple sides: at different times clever and evasive, mystical, ingratiating, studious, and schizophrenic.

Sirhan may be lying about his lack of memory; it is also at least possible that he and his accomplices did stalk RFK, but that the highly suggestible Sirhan had been hypnotically programmed to block memory of the shooting and his associates.

Jack and Bobby conferring

2.10 Who Were the Accomplices?

The LAPD decided not to try to find out. Sirhan's sometimes-stated contention that he killed Kennedy for political reasons, in particular RFK's support for Israel, doesn't hold up well under analysis. For one thing, the TV documentary he cited as provoking him was seen in L.A. on May 20, and Kennedy's speech supporting fighter jets to Israel wasn't given until the 26th. But it was earlier, on May 18, that Sirhan first wrote "RFK must die" over and over in his notebook.

Political views related to the Arab-Israeli conflict may have motivated Sirhan Sirhan. But that motivation was not necessarily that of his accomplices, whoever they were. The tenuous conspiracy leads that exist, including Jerry Owen and perhaps Michael Wayne, point toward right-wing religious extremists, but there is not enough to go on to make any definitive statement. The giddy behavior of the polka-dotted dress girl and her companion seem hardly that of professional killers. But Robert Kennedy had accumulated many powerful enemies during his career - CIA officers, organized crime bosses, Vietnam war hawks, ardent segregationists. Given the fear that Kennedy's achieving the Presidency could induce in them, it is not at all clear who the ultimate sponsors of Sirhan and his accomplices might have been.

2.11 American Tragedy

In his fierce devotion to his older brother Jack, Robert Kennedy earned the moniker "ruthless." His ongoing battles to take down organized crime in America, his haranging of CIA officers to "do more" against Castro, and his willingness to roust executives and journalists out of bed during the 1962 Steel Crisis all contributed to that image. He was feared by many in Washington, at least until Jack took his fateful trip to Dallas in 1963. "Bobby is just another lawyer now," Teamster's president and nemesis Jimmy Hoffa was said to have remarked in the aftermath.

But the "ruthlessness" was always only one side of Bobby Kennedy, the "runt's" tough exterior shell surrounding a sensitive and compassionate core. In the years after his brother's death, he shed the outer shell. Kennedy went to South Africa and spoke against apartheid, he visited the poor in inner cities and in Appalachia, and took on the betterment of poor and disadvantaged people's lives as his cause. It is hard to imagine a starker contrast than there would have been in 1968 between RFK's campaign for social justice, and Richard Nixon's call for "law and order." But that contest was not to be.

In April of 1968, on the way to Indianapolis for a campaign event, Bobby Kennedy learned that Martin Luther King Jr. had been just been killed. Ignoring advice to cancel, Kennedy proceeded and addressed the crowd, telling them at "I have some very sad news for all of you.....Martin Luther King was shot and was killed tonight in Memphis." Expressing kinship with those who felt "hatred and mistrust of the injustice of such an act", RFK said: "I can also feel in my own heart the same kind of feeling," but advocated instead compassion, and went on to quote Aeschylus: "Even in our sleep, pain which cannot forget falls drop by drop upon the heart, until, in our own despair, against our will, comes wisdom through the awful grace of God."

The quote which opened this essay ("If they're going to shoot, they'll shoot") reminds us that Robert Kennedy's journey in his final years was an American version of Greek tragedy. He knew the guns were out there, yet did not veer from the path laid before him.

After his own murder in Los Angeles, Bobby Kennedy's body was put onto a funeral train in New York City, destined for Washington DC and burial in Arlington National Cemetery. For eight hours, the tracks were lined with mourners, saying goodbye to one of the few politicians in America who genuinely championed their cause.

Further Reading

A Lie Too Big to Fail: The Real History of the
Assassination of Robert F. Kennedy
    Lisa Pease, Feral House, 2018

"R.F.K. Must Die!": A History of the Robert
Kennedy Assassination and Its Aftermath
    Robert Blair Kaiser, E.P. Dutton and Co., 1970

Shadow Play
Klaber, William and Melanson, Philip H., St.
Martin's Press, 1997

The Robert F. Kennedy Assassination
Philip H. Melanson, Shapolsky Publishers, Inc.,
1991

The Assassination of Robert F. Kennedy
Christian, Jonn G. and Turner, William G.,
Random House, 1978

The Forgotten Terrorist
Mel Ayton, Potomac Books, 2007

Special Unit Senator
Houghton, Robert A. with Taylor, Theodore,
Random House, 1970

CHAPTER 3
Edward Moore (Ted) Kennedy

3.1 Official Version

The official and highly faked version of the story can be read on Wikipedia:[48]

> The Chappaquiddick incident was a single-vehicle car accident that occurred on Chappaquiddick Island in Massachusetts on Friday, July 18, 1969.[49] The late-night accident was caused by Senator Ted Kennedy's negligence and resulted in the death of his 28-year-old passenger Mary Jo Kopechne, who was trapped inside the vehicle.[50] According to Kennedy's testimony, he accidentally drove his car off the

---

48 https://en.wikipedia.org/wiki/Chappaquiddick_incident

49 https://news.google.com/newspapers?id=eDNWAAAAIBAJ &sjid=p-cDAAAAIBAJ&pg=5310%2C3573743, https://news.google.com/newspapers?id=LJAjAAAAIBAJ&sjid =XqAFAAAAIBAJ&pg=6473%2C231

46 https://news.google.com/newspapers?id=eTNWAAAAIBAJ &sjid=p-cDAAAAIBAJ&pg=4031%2C3668966 https://news.google.com/newspapers?id=s4gsAAAAIBAJ&sjid =x_oDAAAAIBAJ&pg=7143%2C5292039 https://news.google.com/newspapers?id=uYgsAAAAIBAJ&sjid =x_oDAAAAIBAJ&pg=6983%2C700081

one-lane bridge and into the tide-swept Poucha Pond. He swam free, left the scene, and did not report the accident to the police for ten hours; Kopechne died inside the fully submerged car.[51] The car with Kopechne's body inside was recovered by a diver the next day, minutes before Kennedy reported the accident to the police. Kennedy pleaded guilty to a charge of leaving the scene of an accident causing personal injury and later received a two-month suspended jail sentence. The Chappaquiddick incident became national news that likely influenced Kennedy's decision not to campaign for President in 1972 and 1976, and it was said to have undermined his chances of ever becoming President.[52]

---

51 https://news.google.com/newspapers?id=ejNWAAAAIBAJ
    &sjid=p-cDAAAAIBAJ&pg=6816%2C4134699
    https://news.google.com/newspapers?id=bw8hAAAAIBAJ&sjid
    =yXYFAAAAIBAJ&pg=2718%2C310353
52 http://www.nydailynews.com/news/politics/kennedy-legacy-
    chappaquiddick-ted-kennedy-beginning-article-1.398917

3.2 Why the True Chappaquiddick Story Is Impossible to Tell

by Lorraine Boissoneault, April 2, 2018[53]

In 1969, Senator Ted Kennedy careened a car off a bridge, killing passenger Mary Jo Kopechne, but the story of the night's events remain muddled today. Mary Jo Kopechne was 28 years old when she attended a party on Chappaquiddick Island, a tiny spit near Martha's Vineyard, on July 18, 1969. Joined by five of her friends from the 1968 presidential campaign for Sen. Robert F. Kennedy, Kopechne had already made waves in Democratic circles in Washington, working for a Florida senator before moving to Kennedy's Senate staff. She proved herself adept by helping to write an anti-Vietnam War speech for RFK, and helped write the address announcing his ill-fated candidacy for president.

Edward "Ted" Kennedy, meanwhile, was the last surviving son of Joseph Kennedy at the time of the party. After the wartime death of Joseph Jr. and the assassinations of John and Robert, Ted remained as the political leader of the family, a sitting U.S. senator from Massachusetts, with a potential run at the presidency in his future.

---

53 https://www.smithsonianmag.com/history/why-true-story-chappaquiddick-impossible-tell-180968638

As the host of the party in question, Ted brought the women together for a reunion that included Kennedy's cousin, Joseph Gargan, and former U.S. Attorney for Massachusetts Paul Markham. But by the end of the night, the festivities had turned tragic: Kennedy's car overturned on a small bridge and landed upside-down in the water. While Kennedy survived, Kopechne, his passenger, drowned. What happened on that bridge? Was Kennedy drinking and driving? What were he and Kopechne doing together alone in the first place? The details at the time were, as they are now, sparse. It would be a full 10 hours before Kennedy reported the incident to local police.

It's the story of this night that would become an enduring black mark on Kennedy's political career and that serves as fodder for the new film Chappaquiddick, starring Jason Clarke as Ted Kennedy. The scandal haunted him, and the Democratic party, for decades and was also blamed for ruining his presidential prospects. (Kennedy for his part claimed in his autobiography that "it was not a determinant" in his decision to run for president in 1980.)

Senator Edward Kennedy, pictured above on July 22, 1969 after the Chappaquiddick accident that resulted in the death of Mary Jo Kopechne.

Screenwriters Taylor Allen and Andrew Logan felt the drama was the perfect subject for a film about the disposability of women, the impossible expectations of the Kennedy family, how power gets abused, and the role of the media in hiding or exposing political scandal.

Although they don't claim complete veracity for their film—director John Curran says he wasn't interested in making a documentary on the incident—all three men strove to hew as closely as possible to actual events. Logan and Allen based their script on the nearly 1000-page inquest released by the Massachusetts Supreme Judicial Court in 1970.

"The two people who really know what happened that night are dead: Ted and Mary Jo," Curran says. "And the others around them, the ones that are still alive, they aren't going to say anything."

Part of the reason details are so spotty comes from those 10 hours of waiting to report the accident. Why didn't Kennedy contact authorities sooner? He would later claim he was suffering from physical and emotional shock, and not thinking clearly. And then there was talk of a cover-up, of Kennedy and his press team attempting to downplay the incident so as not to harm his future political aspirations.

"Sometimes I'd like to scream a lot but I'm trying to hold it back," said Gwen Kopechne, the mother of Mary Jo, to the Boston Globe. "It would be nice if somebody spoke up." But she also told McCall's Magazine that she believed Kennedy had been behaving erratically after the accident due to shock and a minor concussion. What she didn't understand were how Gargan and Markham, Kennedy's aides who also attempted to retrieve Mary Jo from the car after the accident, didn't report the accident or force Ted to do so.

"Gargan and Markham not only failed to get immediate help, but also let the senator swim back alone to report the accident from Edgartown," the elder Kopechne said. "This is the big hurt, the nightmare we have to live with for the rest of our lives: that Mary Jo was left in the water for nine hours. She didn't belong there."

No one ever provided the answers she wanted. In the immediate aftermath of the car accident, the nation—and the media—were largely distracted by the Apollo 11 moon landing.

"It was the greatest moment in John F. Kennedy's presidential [legacy] happening at the worst possible moment for Ted-Kennedy-the-senator's potential legacy," Allen says. That backdrop of an already distracted news media provided Ted's team with time for damage control, and further obscured the truth about what actually happened.

But once the moon landing receded from the immediate news cycle, the story of Kennedy and Kopechne exploded. Curran and his producers attempted to capture the media coverage by intercutting archival news footage and newspaper headlines throughout the narrative. The film also emphasizes the strain it put on Kennedy's wife, Joan, who was pregnant at the time. She ultimately suffered a miscarriage, which she blamed on the incident. At the same time, she told the wire service United Press International, "I believe everything Ted said." She didn't pay heed to allegations that Kennedy and Kopechne were going for a midnight swim when the accident happened.

This fervor for more details about what exactly happened, and whether some misconduct had occurred between the married men and single women the night of the party, was also experienced by those who attended the party the night of Kopechne's death. Among them were Susan Tannenbaum, who also worked on Robert Kennedy's campaign staff.

"You can't begin to understand what it's been like," Tannenbaum later said. "I place a tremendous value on the right of privacy, but suddenly I'm infamous. The real meaning of what you are and what you value remains intact inside yourself; but there you are splashed all over the papers. How would you feel if a reporter called your mother at 8 a.m. and asked whether she approved of her daughter's conduct in spending the night with a group of married men?"

That aspect of the accident particularly galled the screenwriters. In an era when women were only beginning to enter the workforce in high numbers, press coverage only added to their objectification. "[Kopechne] was an intelligent, strong woman who worked for the Bobby Kennedy campaign in a high capacity and did really great work, including transcribing and then adding to the speech he gave about Vietnam," Allen says.

In the end, Kennedy appeared in court and pleaded guilty to a charge of leaving the scene of an accident. Judge James Boyle sentenced Kennedy to the minimum punishment for the offense, two months' incarceration, but Kennedy never served the jail time, as the judge suspended the sentence.

"He has already been and will continue to be punished far beyond anything this court can impose—the ends of justice would be satisfied by the imposition of the minimum jail sentence and the suspension of that sentence, assuming the defendant accepts the suspension," Boyle said, with the result that the suspension was accepted by the defense team.

No public inquest into the death occurred, and Kennedy went on to make a televised speech about the accident. That speech is one of the few scenes in which the writers of Chappaquiddick took liberties with the facts of the case. In the movie, Kennedy cousin Joe Gargan unsuccessfully tries to convince Ted to read a resignation letter rather than going on television. "We have no evidence in the research to back that up, although it's evident that it was considered," Allen says.

Since then, the Chappaquiddick incident has been used repeatedly as a go-to insult by conservative politicians, particularly when one of their own came under the microscope of a D.C.-scandal. Faith Whittlesey, a Pennsylvania Republican and White House staff member under President Reagan, recalled thinking the incident would be "the end of Kennedy," and that he could be blocked from the presidency for the rest of his career. The story was occasionally resurrected to point to the questions that remained unanswered, even as Kennedy remained in the Senate until his death in 2009.

Though Curran was nervous about taking on someone whose political achievements he admired (especially since there continue to be numerous conspiracy theories about the accident, including that a third person was in the car), he felt the task to be a necessary one.

"Whether you're on the left or right side of the aisle, it's imperative that we take a pretty hard, unvarnished look at our heroes these days," Curran says. "The time is done to let all these guys skate by. I think if this story happened now, it would overshadow the moon landing."

But in 1969, the reverse proved true. The closing scene of Chappaquiddick features a bit of archival footage, from a man-on-the-street style interview in Boston. A reporter asks one person after another whether they would still consider voting for Kennedy after the Chappaquiddick accident. They answer, many resoundingly, with a "yes".

3.3 Nikkolò's First Impressions

The circumstances of the Chappaquiddick incident are very suspicious, to say the least. The smashingly victorious presidential candidate looks on as his girlfriend drowns in his own car, impotent to assist her, and worse, *impotent even to try it.*

Nikkolò's personal opinion is that the official story is a fake. What happened that day, is nothing less than a tightly orchestrated character murder of Ted Kennedy. With the present-day military means, specifically, mind control programs, it is but a simple trick to get any person drugged to such extent that she acts as a brainless zombie. The zombie is able to stand and walk, but is not able to take any initiative at all, as the zombie's mind has been set to zero capacity.

Of course, once the drug effect has finished, the zombie resuscitates and is able to defend itself again. Now, the question some readers might come up with, is, "why did Ted never speak about such a scenario?"

The answer is quite simple. The very same mafia that managed to kill JFK and RFK, is and was obviously powerful enough to threaten EMK with the lives of his wife and children, apart from the usual mistress stuff.

Hence, EMK had no choice but to keep his mouth shut as a safe. Or at least, this is what most of the normal people would have done.

Without knowing the details of Ted's blackmail (which are essential to establish the following easy opinion) Ted's having immediately revealed his poisoning and pointed out the murderers of Jack, would have automatically forbidden the blackmailers from executing their threats, as any hit on his family would directly prove Ted right.

CHAPTER 4
John Fitzgerald Kennedy (JJ) jr.

In March 1997, President Kennedy's son, John, Jr., ran a controversial article in his magazine, George. The article was written by Guela Amir, mother of Yigal Amir, the man who assassinated Israeli Prime Minister Yitzhak Rabin in 1995. In the article, Ms. Amir made it quite clear that her son did not act alone. She provided compelling evidence that Rabin's assassination was sponsored by the Israeli government, and that her son had been goaded into shooting the prime minister by an agent provocateur working for Shin Bet, Israel's equivalent of the FBI and Secret Service combined into one agency. ***The motive for the killing was because Rabin was going to give land back to the Palestinians as specified in the Oslo Accords.*** The following is Ms. Amir's article in its entirety, because of its richness on details.

4.1 *"A Mother's Defense"*
by Guela Amir, March 1997[54]

Israeli Prime Minister Yitzhak Rabin looked exhilarated as he made his way down the podium stairs that chilly autumn night. The pro-peace rally that Rabin had just addressed was an unqualified success. Some 100,000 supporters attended, and public attention was briefly deflected from the mounting criticism of his administration.

Rabin's carefree, buoyant demeanor that night seemed to put his bodyguards at ease, and the half dozen or so agents who accompanied him to his limousine in the parking lot behind the stage encircled him only loosely. None of the Shin Bet (General Security Service) agents in the entourage seemed to notice the slight young man leaning casually against one of the government cars.

As Rabin walked past, the young man drew a pistol, slipped into the crowd of towering security agents, and fired three rounds at the prime minister. Two of them hit Rabin's exposed back, and one shot wounded his bodyguard. As the shots rang out, someone at the scene shouted, "Blanks! Blanks!" as if to reassure the others that

---

54 George Magazine, March 1997, p. 138

the bullets were not real. But the shots were not blanks. Rabin, mortally wounded, was rushed to nearby Ichilov Hospital. Curiously, as Leah Rabin was whisked away by car to Shin Bet headquarters, one of the agents assured the prime minister's wife that the gunman had actually used "a toy gun" and that her husband was fine. The reality was that Rabin lay dying in an emergency room.

The gunman was my son Yigal. The shooting seemed to be an open-and-shut case of assassination. An amateur videotape of the event clearly showed Yigal walking up to the prime minister and shooting him. So how could anyone at the scene have thought that Yigal was shooting blanks? Why was another guard so certain that the gun wasn't real? And how is it that minutes after the shooting, even before the details of the incident were broadcast, Israeli TV received a phone call from a man who claimed to represent a right-wing Jewish organization. He confidently declared, "This time we missed. Next time we won't." Other journalists simultaneously received messages on their pagers with the same statement.

Throughout the tense and painful period since the assassination, the answers to these troubling questions have begun to emerge, and they depict what I believe is an unsavory intrigue at the highest levels of government. This is the story of my search for the truth about the Rabin assassination.

I was visiting a friend's home when the first news bulletin about the assassination was broadcast. The report said that a law student "of Yemenite origin" from Bar-Ilan University had shot the prime minister during a peace rally in Tel Aviv. I had heard about the rally but had no reason to think that my son Yigal would be there. Nervously, I ran to my car and drove the short distance home to Herzliyya, a northern suburb of Tel Aviv, my hands shaking with fear all the way. When I pulled up in front of our house I could hear my husband, Shlomo, shouting. He is a religious scribe with a particularly gentle personality. In our more than 30 years of marriage, I have almost never heard him raise his voice. If he was shouting, something was terribly wrong.

My husband grabbed my hand and we stood together, eyes fixed stonily on the television. Within minutes, our other seven children joined us. Relatives and neighbors streamed into our home. Somebody insisted that it couldn't be Yigal, that "Gali" (his nickname) was visiting a friend. But then a broadcast showed a clear image of my son in the custody of the police. There was no mistake: That was my Yigal. As we sat, dazed, in front of the television, a swarm of Shin Bet agents burst into the living room, charged upstairs to Yigal's room, and took it apart from floor to ceiling. In the streets outside, hundreds of neighbors gathered at the edge of our yard. Reporters and television crews soon joined them. My youngest children were crying uncontrollably. The phone rang off the hook that night, and it has not stopped since.

Daybreak brought the peculiar combination of unreality and routine that is painfully familiar to anyone who has experienced a family tragedy. For years I have managed a nursery school in our home for neighborhood children. Forty preschoolers had enrolled that autumn. At 8 A.M. parents began to arrive with their toddlers; all but a few came that day.

Later, the Shin Bet returned to raid the house. Concealed in the rafters, in a backyard shed, and in an underground cache they found weapons and ammunition. The agents seemed to revel in our shock at each new discovery. At one point I asked one of them why he was spending so much time examining several bars of soap found in the house. He showed me the explosives that were hidden inside. And then they arrested my firstborn son, Hagai, on suspicion of being an accomplice in the assassination of Rabin. Several of Yigal's and Hagai's friends and schoolmates were also hauled in for questioning.

I had lived through four wars and the terrifying Iraqi Scud missiles that struck Israel—just miles from our home—during the Persian Gulf War. But the fear I now felt was something entirely different. In wartime we had been part of a brave and unified community; now I felt that it was my family's own battle—that our family stood alone. Politicians and newspaper columnists branded us a family of "religious fanatics" and "extremists," never pausing to distinguish between us and Yigal. Leading the attacks against us was Rabin's former chief of staff Eitan Haber, who showed up at one of the early court hearings for Yigal and announced that he wouldn't leave the "Amir family in peace until the end of [his] days." Haber's pledge helped inspire a new round of telephone harassment against us, and our home was attacked by vandals.

When the news leaked out that my oldest daughter, Vardit, would soon be married, Haber was on her trail. Needless to say, we were in no mood for celebrations, but according to Jewish religious tradition, once a wedding date has been set it cannot be postponed; Vardit's wedding date had been decided on six months earlier. Haber called for protesters to show up by the thousands.

To our amazement, Haber's plan backfired. There was a spontaneous outpouring of sympathy for our family. Gifts began to arrive from anonymous well-wishers. People we did not know called to offer us help. A stranger lent the young couple a new car for their honeymoon. Nearly every one of our invited guests showed up.

In Jewish tradition the righteous are rewarded with a place in the world to come, and those who are sinful are punished until their souls have been cleansed. When I was a little girl, my grandfather, a revered rabbinical sage, would tell me stories about rare individuals whose sins were so grievous that they could not even enter purgatory. Such a soul, termed a dybbuk in Hebrew, is sent back to the earthly realm to repair the spiritual damage it has wreaked. The dybbuk's only hope is to infiltrate and possess the body of a living person and cling tightly to this purer soul in the hope of securing enough credit, through that person's meritorious deeds, to be forgiven for his own misdeeds. In the spring of 1992, a baneful dybbuk took possession of Israel's radical right-wing political movements and almost succeeded in driving them to ruin. This dybbuk's name was Avishai Raviv.

Raviv was a part of Yigal's other world-his world away from home-and I didn't realize what a central role he played in my son's life until his name began cropping up again and again as the Israeli press probed deeper into the Rabin assassination. Avishai Raviv was born in 1967 in Holon, a backwater development town just south of Tel Aviv. He is remembered in Holon as a youngster who made up for his shyness and stuttering by playing practical jokes on his classmates. Raviv's family was not religious and tended to vote Labor. His life changed suddenly and dramatically when, at the age of 16, he attended a lecture by Rabbi Meir Kahane, the fiery leader of the Israeli nationalist Kach movement. Raviv became active in the movement and, under Rabbi Kahane's influence, seemed to undergo a religious awakening that resulted in his embracing traditional Judaism. While on leave

from service in the Israeli army's elite Givati
Brigade, Raviv began attending demonstrations
and other Kach activities.

Subsequent Israeli and foreign media reports
alleged that at some time during or immediately
following his military service, Raviv was recruited
as an informer for the Shin Bet. Raviv, however,
was no ordinary snitch. It was reported that for
five years he initiated, organized, and led dozens
of extremist right-wing activities.

After the November 1990 assassination of
Rabbi Kahane, the Kach movement split into two
factions. Raviv managed to remain active in both.
He consistently appeared at each group's events
and soon became an infamous fixture on the
nightly news. When scuffles broke out with the
police or hostile passersby, Raviv was often in the
center of the trouble and was arrested dozens of
times (although he was rarely charged and never
imprisoned).

While he was active in the various Kach
splinters, Raviv joined the Temple Mount
Faithful, a group that protests for Jewish rights
on the Temple Mount, the Jewish holy site in
Jerusalem upon which Muslims built the Al Aqsa
mosque and the Dome of the Rock shrine. Israelis
must get permission from the police before they
can pray on the mount for fear of violence
between Arabs and Jews, and the Temple Mount
Faithful has responded with protests. Raviv's
attempt to wrest control from the founder of the
group would lead to his expulsion.

Raviv's agitation led to a particularly ugly episode in August 1991 during a protest outside the Tel Aviv office of Israel's Communist party. As Tamar Gozansky, a Communist member of the Knesset (the Israeli parliament), left the building, Raviv charged at her with a large metal flagpole. Gozansky's aide blocked the assault, and a brawl ensued. Photos of a bloodied Raviv limping away from the rally enhanced his stature among the Kahane activists. Raviv was arrested, but it took nearly four years for the case to go to court. He was let off with a mere nine months' probation and a small fine. The decision by Israeli prosecutors to request probation rather than imprisonment seemed curious.

In the meantime, Raviv had enrolled at Tel Aviv University and was busy making trouble on campus. When a Druse student was elected head of the student union (the largely Jewish student body had chosen a Muslim), Raviv publicly accused him of being disloyal to Israel. The university administration brought disciplinary charges against Raviv for racism. Eventually Raviv was expelled from the university-but not before he asked the Office of the Prime Minister to intervene on his behalf Tel Aviv University officials, however, had had enough of his provocations and his appeal was rejected.

Raviv then founded an organization with settlement activist David Hazan, called Eyal (the Jewish Fighting Organization). It was a religious-nationalist youth movement with barely two dozen members at the start. But Raviv devoted all of his energy to recruiting new members. He soon built himself a small but loyal following, made up primarily of religious teenagers. Raviv lured these youngsters with the enticement of violence and rebellion. According to one girl's later testimony, the charismatic Raviv would arrange Sabbath weekend retreats for Eyal members in various Jewish settlements. I believe the cost of these weekends was usually footed by Raviv.

Before long, Raviv was quarreling with Hazan over the group's direction. Hazan thought Raviv went too far at times, and, reportedly, when Raviv started to openly discuss assassinating a prominent Israeli, Hazan resigned. Raviv took over and shaped Eyal into his vision of the militant vanguard of the Israeli Right. His former roommate, Eran Ojalbo, claimed that Raviv was obsessed with obtaining publicity for himself and his small band of followers and developed a real flair for media stunts. On one occasion, Raviv invited a television crew to watch Eyal members training with weapons. On another, he launched a well-publicized leafleting campaign against mixed Jewish-Arab classes in public schools. He and several Eyal teenagers were brought in for police questioning. Leaflets of this sort are illegal in Israel because they're considered racist, and those who are responsible for creating them are often prosecuted. With Raviv, no charges were pressed.

In September 1993, the Rabin government signed the Oslo accords with the Palestine Liberation Organization (PLO). The accords, and the series of terror bombings that followed their implementation, brought thousands of previously apolitical Israelis into the streets and onto the barricades in embittered protest. These neophyte activists poured into the pre-existing right-wing groups and placed themselves at the disposal of experienced organizers such as Avishai Raviv. One of these new activists was my son Yigal.

The election of Labor party leader Yitzhak Rabin as prime minister in 1992 was the climax of an extraordinary political comeback. After four straight national election losses and more than 15 years in the political wilderness, Rabin led the center-left Labor parry to triumph.

Like many Israelis, my husband and I were saddened by Rabin's election, but we sought consolation in the platform upon which he ran: no negotiations with the PLO, no establishment of a PLO state, and no surrender of the strategically vital Golan Heights. If Rabin adhered to his party's declared principles, Israel's basic security needs would be protected.

In utter disregard of Rabin's platform and in defiance of the Israeli law prohibiting contact with the PLO, Labor party emissaries initiated negotiations with the terrorist group. In September 1993, Rabin announced to a stunned nation that he was going to sign an agreement with PLO chairman Yasir Arafat, giving the PLO partial control over Judea, Samaria, and Gaza. He also planned to release jailed terrorists in exchange for a PLO peace pledge.

In Israel, we hoped desperately that peace would emerge. As a wife and a mother, I know the pain and fear of having watched my sons go off to serve the mandatory three years in the Israeli army. I yearn for the day when we can beat our swords into plowshares.

Sadly, the Oslo process did not produce the peace we expected. Within weeks of the White House handshake, the horror began. A Palestinian terrorist drove a car filled with explosives into a bus near the community of Beit-El, wounding 30 people. Next, a Palestinian driving a car filled with explosives pulled up alongside a bus in the northern Israeli city of Afula. The explosion killed eight people and wounded dozens more. On Remembrance Day, a Palestinian suicide bomber boarded a bus in nearby Hadera and blew himself up, killing five and wounding 25. Public support for Rabin and the Oslo process plummeted. Labor had insisted that the agreement would bring Israel untold benefits. But such dreams were shattered by the rude reality of the old Middle East.

At the same time, a dangerous schism was emerging in Israeli society between those who continued to support the peace process and those who opposed it. Faced with widespread public rejection of the Oslo process, an increasingly defensive Rabin and his cabinet ministers responded by forging ahead with policies that did not have the support of the public majority.

The terror continued. On October 19, 1994, in the heart of Tel Aviv, a Hamas bomber blew up a bus, killing 22 passengers and wounding 48. Three weeks later a terrorist riding a bicycle and carrying a knapsack filled with explosives pedaled up to an army checkpoint in Gaza and killed three soldiers. Each week brought more death, violence, and disillusionment. Around our Sabbath dinner table, the one time each week when all of our children were together, there was a growing sense of despair. Yigal once said, almost in tears, "Who cares if you can now take a vacation trip to Jordan if the street outside is running with Jewish blood?" We didn't know how to answer him. But we did not quite understand just how deeply he felt the pain of the massacred victims. We could not imagine that these terrible events were pushing him past the point of no return.

In the summer of 1995, as Rabin entered the fourth and final year of his term, his popularity was rapidly declining and his coalition government had to count on the support of five Arab members in the Knesset for its survival, though he could not be assured of these crucial votes indefinitely. And there was turmoil inside the Labor party itself Rabin had indicated his willingness to surrender most or all of the Golan Heights region to the Syrians, and a handful of Labor members of the Knesset, led by the 1973 war hero Avigdor Kahalani, balked. Recalling how the Syrians had used the Golan from 1949 to 1967 to shell northern Israel, the Kahalani faction announced that it would vote against the government if it sought to surrender the Golan.

Throughout the spring and summer of 1995, Likud leader Benjamin Netanyahu began to rise in the polls. By late summer of 1995, the polls showed that if elections were held at that time, Netanyahu. would be elected prime minister. The polls found that a majority of the nation no longer supported new territorial surrender.

With elections less than a year away, Rabin's career appeared to be on the verge of ruin, and it's my belief that the Labor leadership quietly turned to the security services to help stave off a defeat at the polls.

The dybbuk in our story will now be joined by an authentic spook. Karmi Gillon came from one of Israel's prominent families. His grandfather, Gad Frumkin, had served as a Supreme Court justice during the pre-state years under the British Mandate. Gillon's father, Colin, was Israel's state attorney during the 1950s, and his mother, Saada, was a deputy attorney general. Gillon's brother, Alon, is a judge who serves as the registrar of Israel's Supreme Court. Karmi Gillon forsook the family profession for a career in the Shin Bet. Created shortly after Israel's birth, the Shin Bet is, in effect, the Israeli FBI and Secret Service combined; it is charged with the tasks of gathering domestic intelligence, counterespionage, and protecting diplomats and

VIPs. Control of the Shin Bet is in the hands of the office of the prime minister.

The Shin Bet like the FBI, has had no small share of controversy over the years. During the time that Gillon was rising in its ranks, the Shin Bet was implicated in a series of scandals. The Landau Commission, established in 1987 to investigate the methods of the Shin Bet, found a pattern of perjury spanning almost two decades. It released an 88 page report sharply censured the Shin Bet leadership for having "failed by not understanding that no security operation, however vital, can put its operatives above the law." The commission characterized the Shin Bet's lawlessness as a danger to democratic society.

Karmi Gillon had a unique field of expertise. While most of his fellow agents spent their time combating the threat of Arab terrorism, Gillon was the Shin Bet's resident expert on Jewish extremist groups; he even wrote his master's thesis at Haifa University on the topic in 1990. He was an advocate of cracking down on Jewish nationalist movements and made no secret of his antipathy to the right-wing outlook.

A few months prior to Gillon's appointment as chief of the Shin Bet in February 1995, Avishai Raviv pulled off an extraordinary stunt. Raviv, accompanied by a band of former Kach activists, attempted to stage a demonstration outside Gillon's Jerusalem home to demand his resignation from the Shin Bet. Raviv and two other people were briefly detained as they approached Gillon's house. Raviv told reporters at the scene —I believe he tipped off the press— that the planned demonstration was "to protest that the head of the Shin Bet is being used as a political tool against the right wing."

To some, Raviv's threatening behavior was just further "evidence" that the Jewish Right was a menace that had to be combatted. In fact, Raviv, as it was later alleged, was already serving as an informer for the Shin Bet, and I find it hard to believe that his stunt hadn't been cleared by Gillon himself. Even before Gillon assumed control of the service, Raviv's provocations had become completely unrestrained. According to the Jerusalem Post, a few days after the machine-gunning of 29 Palestinians by Dr. Baruch Goldstein in March 1994 at Hebron's Cave of the Patriarchs, Raviv rented an apartment —directly above the one where Goldstein had lived— in Kiryat Arba. While Kiryat Arba's leaders were denouncing Goldstein, Raviv was boasting about his admiration for him. According to the Post, one of Raviv's splinter groups, DOV [Suppression of Traitors], vandalized a car belonging to the Kiryat Arba council head, Zvi Katzover, and the next day, Eyal took credit for assaulting Katzover's son so seriously that the boy had to be hospitalized. Again, Raviv was not prosecuted.

Raviv was then accepted by Bar-Ilan University, an Orthodox Jewish institution located in Ramat Gan, not far from Tel Aviv. Raviv registered for several history and philosophy courses and also enrolled in the school's Institute for Advanced Torah Studies. It was there, in the spring of 1994, that he met my son Yigal.

By the time summer rolled around, Raviv was sponsoring a paramilitary Eyal summer camp for militant youngsters. Reporters were invited to watch as Raviv ordered his young recruits, armed with automatic weapons, pistols, and knives, to engage in paramilitary drills and martial-arts training.

Throughout 1994, my husband and I were aware that Yigal was becoming increasingly involved in political activities. But as long as his actions were within the law (and to my knowledge, they were) and he kept up his grades (and he did), we saw no reason to object. If Yigal felt that the Oslo process was endangering Israel —and many, many Israelis felt that way— it was his right, even his obligation, to protest.

What we did not know was that Yigal was being drawn into Raviv's netherworld. Raviv was blanketing the campus with extremist posters. He clashed with campus security when some of the more militant notices were taken down by guards. This resulted in a hearing before an academic disciplinary committee that issued a warning: He would be expelled if he caused any more trouble.

In the summer of 1995, Raviv was once more summoned to a disciplinary committee for his activities. Raviv was again let off with a mere warning by the university administration. Acquaintances from that period later told me that he had behaved as if he had protectzia, the Hebrew slang for pull, or influence in high places. The rabbis at the Institute for Advanced Torah Studies, however, had seen enough of Raviv's antics. He was expelled from the institute.

In Hebrew, Yigal means "he will redeem." My second son was born during those first heady years after the Six Day War, when Israel, on the brink of annihilation by the Arab armies, miraculously beat back the enemy and liberated sacred territories that are so central to Judaism and Jewish history: Judea, Samaria, Gaza, the Golan Heights, and, of course, Jerusalem. God had redeemed his nation, and we named our second child Yigal as an affirmation of that miracle. Even as a young child, Yigal displayed an energy and drive that set him apart from other children. Whatever Yigal wanted, he found a way to get. Yigal had never given us a day of trouble in his life. After graduating at the top of his high school class, he began his military service. His fierce patriotism compelled him to volunteer for an elite combat unit. As a mother, I dreaded his decision to serve in the unit that is called into battle first when war breaks out. But how could we stand in the way of our son's desire to defend his country?

When Yigal finished his three mandatory years of service, I detected a new seriousness in him.

He was hired as a government emissary to Latvia, where he taught Hebrew to potential Jewish immigrants to Israel. He subsequently told me that this is where he was trained by the Shin Bet.

Upon his return, Yigal gained admission to law school at Bar-Ilan. For a young man of Yemenitc background, this was quite an accomplishment: Jews from Yemen and other Arab countries start out at the bottom of Israel's socioeconomic ladder, and it has taken decades to break into professions dominated by those of European origin. Yigal enrolled not only in the Bar-Ilan University law school but simultaneously in its computer classes and the university's religious-studies program.

Like many of his fellow students, Yigal was drawn to political activism by the Oslo accords. He attended a number of mass demonstrations in Tel Aviv and Jerusalem and helped organize a number of campus rallies, but he soon despaired of their impact because there was no chance of changing Rabin's mind.

Yigal found himself overwhelmed by a sense of frustration, and this helped to pave the way for his association with Raviv. He was now spending a good deal of his time organizing Sabbath weekend retreats for student activists in various Israeli towns and in the settlements. As Yigal's friends told me subsequently, he and Raviv worked together, publicizing the retreats, preparing literature for the discussion groups and seminars, and arranging for guest lecturers.

We hardly saw Yigal during the summer and early autumn of 1995. 1 couldn't imagine how he mustered the energy for such outings after his grueling schedule of classes. But if he was using his day and a half off from school (Israel's weekends last only from Friday afternoon until Saturday night) for educational purposes, we considered it worthwhile.

According to Yigal's friends and others who have since testified in court, Raviv seemed to be obsessed with one topic: killing Rabin. He and Yigal frequently engaged in discussions about the feasibility of assassination.

On September 16, Israeli television broadcast what was purported to be a secret late-night swearing-in ceremony organized by Eyal. At the ceremony, which was later revealed to have been staged for the television cameras, Raviv assembled what he claimed were a group of new Eyal recruits at the graves of pre-state Jewish underground fighters, according to the Jerusalem Post.

Raviv scored his biggest media triumph on October 5,1995, when the opposition political parties organized a mass rally in downtown Jerusalem to protest the mounting Arab terror and the government's weak response. Although I rarely attended demonstrations, Yigal and I went to, this one together. The main speaker that Saturday night was Likud leader Benjamin Netanyahu. Circulating among the huge crowd was Avishai Raviv and his band of Eyal hotheads.

According to the Jerusalem Post, Raviv had given them handouts depicting Prime Minister Rabin dressed up in an SS uniform. When demonstrators urged the Eyal sign holders to remove the offensive placards, they refused. Eyal's founder, David Hazan, passed by and tore up one of the posters. A gang of Eyal toughs promptly pummeled him.

The Post reported that an Israeli television reporter, Nitzan Chen, later revealed that Raviv had approached him and urged him to broadcast the sign on the nightly news report, and that he had even called later to be sure that it had been included.

In the Knesset the next morning, the Labor party made good use of the poster. Netanyahu was accused of having failed to condemn them. It helped reinforce the notion that the Likud was extremist and irresponsible. In a radio interview shortly afterward, Rabin told the public that "the Likud provides extremists with inspiration. It cannot wash its hands of this and claim it has nothing to do with it."

Netanyahu's request to meet with Rabin to attempt to ease the mounting political tensions was ignored. Rabin's refusal to even meet with the Likud leader again strengthened the idea that Netanyahu was beyond the pale. It also helped deflect public attention away from Arab terrorism. Finally, so it seemed, Rabin had found an effective campaign strategy.

On November 4, 1995, Yigal exited a bus and
made his way toward Malchei Yisrael Square,
where thousands of supporters had already
assembled. The large floodlights placed outside
the Tel Aviv city hall illuminated the area for
many blocks, and security was stepped up around
the demonstration. On hand were more than 700
police and border-patrol officers, dozens of
undercover police, and agents of the Shin Bet who
had been assigned the job of guarding the
featured political leaders.

The gathering, whose theme was "Yes to peace,
no to violence," had been heavily advertised for
weeks. Labor party-dominated municipalities and
unions pulled out all stops in their drive to
generate a large turnout for the rally. Some of
the biggest names in Israeli entertainment were
recruited to perform. In addition to Prime
Minister Rabin and Foreign Minister Peres, other
top Labor leaders were present. It was meant to
be an impressive show of strength for the party
and proof positive that large segments of the
country still supported the peace process.

Yigal strode quickly through the crowd. The
police had erected special metal railings to keep
the crowd away from the rostrum, but people
were simply walking around the barriers. When
Yigal arrived near the stage he circled around the
police line and descended the stairway that led to
the cordoned parking area, where the limousines
of the prime minister and other government
officials were parked.

After a while, a Shin Bet agent approached and asked Yigal who he was. He reportedly replied that he was one of the drivers. The agent apparently accepted the answer and walked away. At no point did anyone ask Yigal to produce identification or seriously challenge his presence near the cars. Much criticism was later leveled against the police and the Shin Bet for failing to create a "sterile" area near the stage, a standard security precaution.

Yigal struck up a conversation with some of the drivers and police officers who were mingling in the parking lot. Later they would admit that they had assumed he was either an undercover policeman or one of the entertainers' drivers. From his position in the parking lot, Yigal could clearly hear the singing of the performers.

As the speeches and performances continued on the stage above him, Yigal bided his time. He did not check his watch, nor did he display any anxiety, he told me. He said that if the police had stopped him or seriously questioned him at this stage, he would have taken it as a sign from above and abandoned the plan to kill Rabin. But on this evening there were no such actions by the police or Shin Bet agents. And so Yigal was content to peacefully wait for the rally to end and the prime minister to be escorted to his car.

In the chaotic aftermath of the assassination, rival Israeli law-enforcement officials engaged in a frenzy of finger-pointing and recriminations. In the newspapers and on the airwaves, the Police

Ministry and the Shin Bet hurled accusations at one another, each attempting to blame the other for the lax security. Shin Bet head Karmi Gillon, whose name was then a state secret, announced that the security services would conduct an internal investigation. The police announced their own internal probe. Astonishingly, within 48 hours —on November 7— the Shin Bet report was concluded and leaked to the press. The document, which was authored by three former branch heads of the Shin Bet, found that the entire protection system assigned to the prime minister had collapsed. The report lambasted the inability of the Shin Bet to gather intelligence on extreme right-wing groups. After the report's release, the head of the protection department, identified as "D," was forced to resign. The Shin Bet insisted that D's negligence was the sole reason for the procedural breaches on the night of the killing.

On Tuesday, November 7, Raviv was arrested by the police, on charges that he was involved in the assassination. The Jerusalem Post asserted that his group, Eyal, was being investigated in connection with a conspiracy to kill the prime minister. As the handcuffed Raviv was brought to court under heavy police guard, he yelled to reporters, "This is a political investigation and a false arrest! This is a dictatorship!"

The next day, the government announced the formation of a commission of inquiry into the assassination, to be headed by former Supreme

Court justice Meir Shamgar. And from the outset, the Shamgar Commission was plagued by conflicts of interest and questions of impartiality. Shamgar himself had served for many years as Judge Advocate General of the Israeli army and maintained ties to the military establishment. He was also a close personal friend of the Rabin family. Shamgar was joined on the panel by a former head of the Mossad, Zvi Zamir, and Professor Ariel Rosen-Zvi, dean of Tel Aviv University law school. Professor Rosen-Zvi was in the advanced stages of cancer at the time and would be dead within weeks of the commission's final report.

In a strange twist, Judge Alon Gillon, the older brother of Shin Bet head Karmi Gillon, was named secretary of the commission. Sitting in on the commission's proceedings was the brother of the government official who was most likely to be blamed if the commission concluded that the Shin Bet had failed to safeguard Rabin. The possible conflict of interest apparently escaped the notice of the commissioners — Karmi Gillon would testify before the commission at length. Unfortunately, neither the public nor the news media were allowed to attend many of the commission's hearings.

Equally troubling was the presence of Attorney General Michael Ben-Yair. Since the commission was investigating, among other issues, whether the attorney general's office was granting some Shin Bet informants —one of which was later alleged to be Raviv— immunity from prosecution, the presence of the attorney general at the hearings was surprising indeed. If the government's intent was to definitively ascertain what led to Rabin's assassination, then even the perception of impropriety should not have been tolerated.

During the days following the assassination, Attorney General Ben-Yair had ordered a crackdown on individuals who were suspected of engaging in "inflammatory speech." Curiously, the crackdown continued for several weeks, then stopped suddenly. Ben-Yair announced —in a stunning reversal— that mere words could not cause an individual to engage in criminal acts, and they had not caused Yigal's act. "The person who killed the prime minister did not do so under the influence of incitement.... He acted due to a complete worldview, which he had developed.... It wasn't because of a poster here or there." Ben-Yair was not the only one to engage in a sudden, unexplained about-face. Police Minister Moshe Shahal, who had previously declared, "We believe that a group of people carefully prepared the ground to conspire to murder carefully chosen targets," now asserted that Yigal was a lone gunman who had organized the assassination on his own.

But the "inciting rhetoric" and "organized conspiracy" theories had served their purpose they had inflamed public opinion against the Israeli Right. Now, I believe they needed to be discarded lest they open an even bigger can of worms about incitement and conspiracy.

On the weekend before the Shamgar Commission was to hear its first witness, Karmi Gillon, there was a stunning revelation: Israeli television and radio both reported that Raviv was, indeed, an undercover agent for the Shin Bet. According to the reports, Raviv, codenamed "Champagne" by his Shin Bet handlers, had been on the government's payroll for at least two years as a top infiltrator of the far Right. But according to an investigation by the Jerusalem Post, Raviv's task involved much more than infiltration: His orders were to attract individuals to Eyal, incite them to illegal activities, and then inform on them to the Shin Bet.

One of the sources of this information was Rabbi Benny Elon, the dean of Yeshivat Beit Orot, a religious college, and son of a retired Supreme Court justice. Elon would later become a Knesset member in 1996. This prominent Jewish-settlement activist and leader of the right-wing group Moledet held a press conference and charged that Raviv had effectively manufactured the wild far Right. He was, in Elon's words, an "agent provocateur," carrying out a mission by the government to discredit the right-wing opposition, including, by association, the Likud. "I would venture to say," Elon added, "that the whole organization [Eyal] and its activities, including the poster depicting Rabin in an SS uniform, were all paid for by the Shin Bet." (The Shin Bet later denied the charge.) Elon went on to say, "There is a reasonable suspicion that [Raviv's activity] was okayed by the legal authority."

Elon, who had met Raviv and other Eyal activists on a number of occasions at demonstrations and elsewhere, said that Raviv had been Yigal's constant companion in the months prior to the killing. How could Raviv have been so close to Yigal and not known, as Raviv later claimed in court, of the assassination plan? And how could a Shin Bet informer have been so closely involved in all of these activities without the knowledge of the Shin Bet, which is supervised by the Office of the Prime Minister?

The two weeks after the assassination were the most horrible period of my life. Now, suddenly, came the revelation of a Shin Bet connection to Yigal's "pal" Raviv.

The Likud, which had been on the defensive since the assassination, came to life in the wake of the Raviv-Shin Bet accusations. At a meeting of the Likud executive bureau, Netanyahu called for "a full, thorough, and exhaustive investigation into the Raviv affair. There must be no coverup. Even if only a fraction of the provocative activities attributed to Raviv are true, they constitute a grave danger to democracy. There must be an investigation, and it must come now, with no delays and no excuses."

And then there were more revelations. Israel's leading daily, Yediot Ahronot, reported that in testimony before a closed session of the Shamgar Commission, several young women at a religious seminary said that they had recognized Yigal and Raviv from a Sabbath retreat at Ma'aleh Yisrael the previous summer. The girls told their teacher, Sarah Eliash, that Raviv had denounced several Rabin government officials as "traitors." During several marathon ideological discussions that weekend, Raviv had attempted to goad Yigal into killing Rabin, ridiculing his "cowardice" for not being willing to assassinate a "traitor." In court, Raviv said he had heard Yigal talk about the "need to kill Rabin" but claimed he hadn't taken him seriously.

The girls testified: "We used to see Raviv and Amir on Saturdays during last summer. These gatherings were arranged by Yigal. We would sit out on a hilltop there. There were no demonstrations or any violence. They were basically study groups. We met, like, several times.... Raviv was real macho. He kept saying to Yigal, 'You keep talking about killing Rabin. Why don't you do it? Are you frightened? You say you want to do it. Show us that you're a man! Show us what you are made of"' The girls testified that Yigal didn't react at all to Raviv's pressure and just changed the subject of discussion.

Suddenly, information about Raviv was spilling forth. Raviv's former roommate in Kiryat Arba, and former member of Eyal, Eran Ojalbo, testified as a witness for the defense at Yigal's trial. He revealed that Raviv had said that Rabin was a rodef—the Hebrew term for someone who endangers others and therefore should be killed. At a weekend retreat organized by Yigal in the settlement of Ma'alch Yisrael, press reports say, Raviv had marked several different government leaders for death.

Ojalbo also testified that ten minutes after news of the assassination had been announced, Raviv called him and asked how he was and if he knew who had shot Rabin. Ojalbo responded that in television reports he had seen that it was "a short Yemenite guy." Raviv asked if it was Yigal. "I looked again," Ojalbo testified, "and said that it was Yigal."

Ojalbo also maintained that Raviv had verbally pressured Yigal to attempt an assassination of Rabin. "Raviv told Yigal and others, time and time again, that there was a din-rodef [judgment] on Yitzhak Rabin. He said, 'Rabin should die,' and whoever killed him was a righteous person.... Raviv had a powerful influence on Yigal. He continuously emphasized to him and other students that whoever implemented the din-rodef against Rabin was carrying out a holy mission."

Israel television's Chen appeared before the Shamgar Commission and related the details of Raviv's involvement with the SS handouts. Raviv's job was to discredit the Right, Chen said, and what could be more effective than giving the public the idea that the entire opposition considered Rabin to be a Nazi?

The next Raviv revelation came from the Jerusalem Post investigative reporter Steve Rodan. He reported that "Israel Broadcasting Authority spokesman [Ayala Cohen] said the first report of the Rabin shooting was broadcast at 9:48 P.M. Channel 1 began broadcasting live at 10:15, and 15 minutes later, the alleged assassin was identified as a 25-year-old student from Herzliyya."

But Rodan also wrote that Raviv had arrived at the Tel Aviv rally 15 minutes before Rabin's murder. When the first rumors of the shooting swept through the crowd, at 9:50 P.M., Rodan reported, "Immediately Raviv pulled out his mobile telephone and spoke to an unidentified person. 'He called somebody,' one of the witnesses said. 'He asked whether they shot Rabin.' Then Raviv asked, 'Was he hurt?'.... When he finished [the conversation] he shouted, 'It was Yigal. Don't you know Yigal? He was at the Orient House demonstrations [Eyal's protests at PLO headquarters in Jerusalem].' Raviv then made his way toward nearby Ichilov Hospital and then disappeared."

"Those around him could not understand how Raviv knew the identity of the assassin before anyone else," Rodan reported.

As the accusations about Raviv mounted, the opposition Tsomet party petitioned the High Court of Justice to prevent Attorney General

Ben-Yair from attending further Shamgar Commission hearings. The petition asked that, at a minimum, Ben-Yair be prohibited from questioning witnesses, including Shin Bet agents and confidential informants, whose activities he might have authorized. The petition also argued that since Ben-Yair might himself be called to testify, it was improper for him to become familiar with others' testimony.

Instead of ruling on the merits of the petition, the High Court offered a compromise proposal under which Tsomet would withdraw its petition in exchange for a promise that Ben-Yair would absent himself if a conflict of interest arose. But it was a disappointing action by the Court, and it did little to restore the image of the commission. The growing public perception was that Ben-Yair was sitting in on the commission hearings to conduct damage control for the government in the wake of the Raviv-Shin Bet revelations.

On December 14, Raviv himself appeared before the Shamgar Commission. After completing his secret testimony, he was whisked away in a government car and vanished from public view.

Following Raviv's testimony, the commission issued warning letters to six Shin Bet officials, including Karmi Gillon. The letters cautioned the officials that they might face criminal liability as a result of their involvement with the events surrounding Raviv and the Rabin murder. Gillon and several other Shin Bet agents were called back for additional testimony, in light of Raviv's statements to the commission.

On January 8, 1996, Karmi Gillon resigned. The Israeli media concluded that had he not stepped down voluntarily, the Shamgar Commission would have insisted on his removal. The man who had been championed as an expert on Jewish extremism had failed to examine and follow up on information that he had received regarding a possible attack on the prime minister by Jewish extremists. But what was widely perceived as Gillon's negligence explained only a fraction of the events that led to the assassination. Why hadn't the Shin Bet ordered Raviv to cease his provocations? Why had it not detained or at least questioned Yigal before he acted? Why the strange restraint in the face of a threat to the prime minister?

The Jerusalem Post reported: "Yigal told investigators that he acted alone, did not belong to an extremist organization, and had 'received instructions from God to kill Prime Minister Rabin.'" Yigal also reiterated in court that he acted alone. I believe he did so in order not to implicate others.

On March 28, 1996, the Shamgar Commission released its report. Of the 332 pages, 118 were declared classified. The unclassified parts blamed Gillon for the failures of the Shin Bet on the night of the murder but did not find him or any other agents criminally negligent. According to the Jerusalem Post, the unclassified sections contained only a few scattered references to the relationship between the running of agents and the Shin Bet. The report depicted the assassination as a failure by the agents protecting Rabin to organize themselves effectively. In one of its least believable conclusions, the Shamgar report claimed that Gillon —the expert on right-wing Jewish extremism— "did not conduct even one substantive, relevant, thorough, and comprehensive discussion with all the security and intelligence-gathering bodies to review methods." This was after two senior Shin Bet officers told the commission that they had gathered intelligence reports that right-wing groups could be a threat to both Jews and Arabs.

Equally bizarre was the commission's assertion that in order to "safeguard" the Shin Bet's operational methods, testimony by or about Raviv and his role had to be placed in a classified appendix to the report. In Chapter 5 of the commission's report is a section entitled "The Avishai Raviv Episode." The page is blank except for the cryptic note that "the details of this subject will be discussed in the secret appendix."

A section entitled "The Operation of Agents" states: "The body that operates an informer must keep tight control of him and not allow him to initiate actions at his will ... and to prevent the carrying out of provocations that in the end might have a boomerang effect." Could they have been referring to Raviv?

The official investigation of Raviv's relationship with Yigal remains shrouded in secrecy. Labor, of course, wanted no further probing into a potentially explosive scandal. Ironically, Likud, having forced national elections in two months, preferred to put the issue to rest.

The idea of using an agent provocateur was not originated by the Shin Bet. The secret police in czarist Russia created fake anarchist cells in order to attract genuine anarchist militants whom they would arrest and execute. When the Soviets came to power, they employed the same tactic against their political enemies. In the United States, the FBI created COINTELPRO (the counterintelligence program) to recruit potential lawbreakers, help incite them to break the law, then arrest them. By the late 1970s, the use of such unscrupulous tactics had been exposed and widely condemned as improper interference with citizens' rights. In Israel, unfortunately, dirty tricks are still commonly used.

Neither the Shin Bet nor the political echelon that controls it, the Office of the Prime Minister, seems to have appreciated the difference between a legitimate informant and an agent provocateur.

I believe Raviv enjoyed the full backing and protection of the Shin Bet. He assaulted a member of the Knesset and did not serve a day in jail. The Office of the Prime Minister was contacted to help intervene in an attempt to prevent his expulsion from Tel Aviv University. He emerged scot-free from distributing racist literature, publicly praising Baruch Goldstein, holding illegal summer militia camps, and allegedly distributing the Rabin-SS poster. On many occasions, he allegedly urged the assassination of Rabin and other Labor government officials and was never prosecuted. Raviv's lawlessness had to have sent the message to potential extremists that violence could be employed with impunity.

As I see it, Karmi Gillon and Avishai Raviv were the perfect match: Gillon, the Shin Bet chief obsessed with the belief that right-wing Jewish terrorist groups were on the loose; and Raviv, the alleged Shin Bet informer actively ensuring that Gillon's dark prophesies came true. If Raviv was an informer, did he alert Shin Bet agents that Yigal was now a potential assassin? I find it inconceivable that he would have kept such information to himself. Yet Yigal was never arrested. Never questioned. Never had his gun license revoked. Never had his gun confiscated. Did Gillon know from Raviv about Yigal's activities? If so, why didn't he order his agents to undertake any action against Yigal? What were they waiting for?

Just minutes after Yigal had shot the prime minister, somebody called reporters, identified himself as a spokesman for a right-wing organization, and claimed, "This time we missed. Next time we won't." It seems astonishing to me that the caller could have known that the shots were fired by a right-wing Jew rather than an Arab. Why did he think that the attack had failed?

Could the caller have been Raviv? I think he spent months inciting Yigal to make the attempt. He may have suspected that it would take place that night. I also think that he positioned himself at the rally, close enough to the scene of the crime to know that the shots had been fired, enabling him to make the immediate calls to the reporters. (One wonders what might emerge from an investigation of the itemized bill of Raviv's cellular phone.)

Yet, for some reason, Raviv was sure that the attempt would fail. Why? Perhaps somebody — either Raviv or someone else— was surreptitiously supposed to have disabled Yigal's gun, either by removing the firing pin or by replacing the bullets with blanks, before the shooting. It has been claimed in court that it was Yigal who shouted, "Blanks! Blanks!" But Shin Bet agents are trained to shout out "Blanks! Blanks!" in security drills. And I believe that that cry, combined with the fact that an agent assured Mrs. Rabin that the gun was not real, might mean that the Shin Bet were expecting an unsuccessful assassination attempt.

The Shin Bet could have arrested Yigal at any time in the weeks before the rally and charged him with plotting to kill Rabin. But the impact on the public would be so much more dramatic if Shin Bet agents heroically foiled an attempt on the prime minister's life. But something went terribly wrong. The bullets were not blanks; the gun was not a toy.

My belief has some basis in past events. Foiling attempted crimes at the last second is a well-established Shin Bet method. In April 1984, in a Shin Bet operation, agents were tracking a group of settlement leaders who were engaged in retaliatory attacks against Arab terrorists. They followed the suspects as they planted explosives on several Arab buses in East Jerusalem. After this, the suspects were allowed to travel back to their residences. Only then did the Shin Bet raid their houses and conduct arrests. At the time, it was reported that the Shin Bet delayed taking suspects into custody until after the bombs were planted in order to sensationalize their own heroic efforts. Faced with the shocking news story, then prime minister Yitzhak Shamir had no choice but to let the security services arrest dozens of other suspects and crack down on the settlement organizations.

More recently, there is the disturbing case of the Kahalani brothers, Eitan and Yehoyada, from Kiryat Arba. The two men were convicted of plotting to shoot an Arab in retaliation for the murder of a Jewish settler. The pair had taken their loaded rifles to a road near the village of Kafr Batir, where they spotted an Arab man on a bicycle. As the Arab approached their truck, Eitan raised his rifle to fire, but the gun malfunctioned and Shin Bet agents waiting in ambush rushed to arrest the two brothers. The charge sheet is revealing. It contends that the murder was dramatically foiled "as a result of the removal of the firing pin by GSS [Shin Bet] without prior knowledge of the accused, [hence] no shot was fired."

The Kahalanis' attorney argued that a third individual involved in planning the attack was a Shin Bet plant who had disabled the guns. The alleged informant was arrested and then quickly released despite the charge that he was involved in the conspiracy. Why did the Shin Bet wait until after Eitan Kahalani had pulled the trigger to move in and make the arrest?

What Israel needs now is to heal the terrible wounds that the nation has suffered as a result of the assassination and its aftermath. To ease the malaise that is eating away at our society. To restore the public's confidence in our government. And, above all, to preserve the principles that are the basis of our democratic way of life.

My concern for the lives and the freedom of my two sons ensures that I will not rest until the truth —about Avishai Raviv, the Shin Bet and my son Yigal— is fully revealed.

4.2 JJ Told Who Murdered His Father But Nobody Was Paying Attention (I)

by Jane Grey, 12 August 2016[55]

Most people think that from the day he saluted his father's casket at just three years old, till the evening his plane went down, JFK Jr. just went about his business, playing the game of life-like everyone else.

After all, he did live, for the most part, a relatively ordinary life, in spite of being the Prince of America's Camelot. So, what do you suppose was going on in the mind of the sexiest man alive? He could have written his own political ticket, yet he went into publishing. Many expected him to land in politics and most likely were a bit perplexed when he decided to publish a magazine instead.

---

55 http://www.yogaesoteric.net/content.aspx?lang=EN&item=9829
http://robscholtemuseum.nl/jane-grey-jfk-jr-told-the-world-who-murdered-his-father-but-nobody-was-paying-attention/

JFK Jr. launches his "George" magazine

Some thought he was afraid to go into politics because of the "Kennedy Curse". However, nothing could be further from the truth. What he did proved to be more dangerous than any political arena, and he knew that from the start. But...John-John had a mission...and that mission was to expose the villain who orchestrated that "dastardly act" upon his father.

Unbeknownst to the public, John-John was digging deep for proof. And, how else could he expose the truth when all the media outlets were controlled by the very cabal he planned to expose?

Enter..."George"

When he presented his magazine, "George", to the world, he was, for all practical purposes, signing his own death warrant. "George" was a veiled threat...in a symbolic sort of way. How many men named "George" comes to mind at just the thought of President John F. Kennedy's so called assassination? One for sure: George Bush Sr.

The cabal wanted his father dead, that is a fact, but the namesake of John F. Kennedy, Jr.'s magazine...their minion, arranged it. And...once he had the proof, the truth would come out in his very own magazine.

"As President, John F. Kennedy understood the predatory nature of private central banking. He understood why Andrew fought so hard to end the Second Bank of the United States. So Kennedy wrote and signed Executive Order 11110 which ordered the US Treasury to issue a new public currency, the United States Note.

Kennedy was working with President Soekarno of Indonesia who was at that time the signatory for the Global Collateral Accounts which were intended to be used for humanitarian purposes but which were subverted at the time of the Bretton-Woods agreement at the end of WWII.

The intention of Kennedy and Soekarno was to end the reign of the globalist privately owned central banking system – which is the main reason that Kennedy was killed, and for his part

Soekarno remained under house arrest for the rest of his life." (Excerpt from: All Wars Are Bankers' Wars).

There was a rumor that John-John had obtained the proof he needed and an expose' was in the works, until his untimely, and mostly "suspicious," death. Of course, the media campaigned that he was an irresponsible thrill seeker; but then they would, wouldn't they? Although many people knew JFK, Jr. was murdered; and they were right about who was responsible...they were just wrong about the reason.

Future President John Fitzgerald Kennedy wearing his US Navy uniform

John Jr. was warned by family members about the risks involved in his pursuit. But, he was determined to get justice for his father and bring truth to light, exposing the darkness that shrouds our planet. So ask yourself...what would you do, if you were a mere babe when your father, who just happened to be the most important man in the country, was murdered in such a gruesome manner, and you never had the opportunity to know him...would you just let it go?[56]

4.3 JJ Told Who Murdered His Father But Nobody Was Paying Attention (II)

by Jane Grey, September 2016[57]

Bush's association with the CIA's Cubans was already widely known. Fletcher Prouty knew and wrote of it. Fabian Escalante, the head of Cuban counter intelligence, knew and has written about it. James Files, who claims very credibly, to have been a driver for the Mafia shooters in Dallas, has spoken on-camera about it. And FBI director J. Edgar Hoover, knew about it and wrote about it in his memo. So Bush was already a suspect in Hoover's eyes. The CIA planners, then, would not

---

56   I omit the rest of the quote, because it centers on JFK instead of on JFK jr.

57   http://yogaesoteric.net/content.aspx?lang=EN&item=9853

have told anyone else, "in case you get arrested, tell the cops you're an independent oil man from Houston". They would not have done this, since it would tend to incriminate Bush, who was already in a highly visible, highly suspicious position.

Another unlikely possibility is that this "independent oil operator from Houston" was just some innocent oil operator, who somehow managed to attract suspicion, and was arrested. Do you think it's possible that another oil man from Houston just happened to be in that corner of Dealey Plaza? As unlikely as it seems, if you think it was possible, then certainly Bush would have been reasonable in thinking that, as he was being arrested, there were other independent oil operators in the crowd who witnessed his arrest.

Bush spoke to a group of oil men in Dallas the night before the assassination. If it were possible that some of them were in Dealey Plaza, he would need to be terrified of the possibility that some of them might actually have seen the arrest, and would have been able to identify him as the object of that arrest.

No wonder, then, that Bush freaked out, and made this stupid incriminating phone call to the FBI. Even if it showed that he was not in Houston, or in the Caribbean, but in Dallas, at least it suggested that he was not in police custody for the murder of the President, in Dealey Plaza. But now stop and think a minute: Why was he arrested? What was he doing that drew this cop's attention at all? What could he possibly have been doing to make this cop think that he needed to arrest Bush?

Perhaps walking out of a building without attracting attention is harder than it sounds; and it reasonable to suppose that the crowd outside the Dal-Tex building had heard the shots, had heard that the President had been wounded, and they were carefully scrutinizing anyone who came out of the building.

But this story shows clearly that Bush was not the sort of cold-blooded killer who could take part in the murder of a man, and then act and look like nothing was going on as he tried to leave the scene of the crime. And it turns out that as an old man, Bush continues to suffer from this character trait, of being unable to hide feelings that need to be kept secret.

As you can see below, at Gerry Ford's funeral, Bush suddenly breaks into a wide grin while speaking of the Kennedy assassination. This is not a Mona Lisa smile. This is face-wrenching spasm of glee.

[During the rest of the speech Bush has a serious facial expression.] Why would Bush grin at his recollection of watching John Kennedy's brains splatter? The point for us now is that he apparently had a similarly inappropriate, show-stopping expression on his face as he attempted to exit the Dal-Tex building; he had the look of a murderer in his eye, so clearly that it could not be missed; as this funeral-grin could not be missed.

Bush' sudden grin upon mentioning the JFK Shooting

And the guilt plastered all over Bush's face drew people's attention. And this cop, Vaughn, arrested him. Now remember, Roger Craig tells this story in the context of his discussions with New Orleans District Attorney Jim Garrison about the suspects who were arrested that day and who then evaporated without leaving a mugshot, interview, fingerprint, or name. Garrison spoke not only to Roger Craig, but he no-doubt spoke to Vaughn, who made the arrest. And Garrison adds the following, in the book On the Trail of the Assassins:

"At least one man arrested immediately after the shooting had come running out of the Dal-Tex Building and offered no explanation for his presence there. Local authorities hardly could avoid arresting him because of the clamor of the onlookers. He was taken to the Sheriff's office, where he was held for questioning. However, the

Sheriff's office made no record of the questions asked this suspect, if any were asked; nor did it have a record of his name. Later two uniformed police officers escorted him out of the building to the jeers of the waiting crowd. They put him in a police car, and he was driven away. Apparently this was his farewell to Dallas, for he simply disappeared forever."

This vision of the panicked Bush being arrested, no-doubt terrified as he was taken to the police station, and possibly even booked (though the record of any such booking has been destroyed) provides a context that explains a number of Bush's otherwise-mysterious actions. Certainly Bush was freaked out and panic-stricken! An angry crowd clamored for his arrest, and jeered his release. Being a newbie in these dark affairs, Bush didn't have confidence in the ability of the old devils at CIA to make water run uphill, to make time run backwards, to silence the witnesses, to destroy the records, and make it all go away. And so he panicked; he acted on his own, stupidly; he called the FBI, thinking that he was "cleverly" providing evidence that it wasn't him who was arrested in front of the Dal-Tex building that day.

In his panic-stricken state, this seemed like a good idea. He was unable to see that he was actually creating a permanent and absolutely positive record of his involvement. We can now also explain the grin. He grins ridiculously at Gerry Ford's funeral, at the mention of John

Kennedy's murder, not because he is such a ghoul that he thinks splattering the contents of Kenney's head all over Jackie Kennedy was funny; but because mentioning the assassination causes him to recall the comedy of errors that produced his own ridiculous panic, arrest, more panic, and so on. Garrison wrote his paragraph about Bush's arrest in 1988. Deputy Craig's article was written in 1971 and posted in 1992. But the significance of these paragraphs was discovered last week. There hardly was an internet in 1992 when Craig's article was posted. And for 19 years, no one noticed that this phrase, "independent oil man from Houston", is a very unique description of Bush. No one noticed until last month, when one of the moderators of "JFKMurderSolved" discovered it. So the pieces continue to fall into place. Little by little, the picture is filled in, the questions get answered. And the conclusions become more incontrovertible. This is just the sort thing that happened with the theory of Evolution and the Big Bang theory (...). And someday they may start to teach history, as a science, based on evidence, in the universities. Really! It could happen! At which point, Bush's involvement in JFK's murder will be taught, like evolution, as the only plausible explanation of the available reliable evidence.

Until recently, Bush had nothing more to say about his whereabouts the day of the assassination than that he doesn't remember where he was. That in itself is extraordinarily incriminating. Everyone who was alive at the time remembers where they were on 9-11, and on the day Kennedy was murdered. But, saying that he doesn't remember, however improbable, is at least consistent with Bush's autobiography, which mentions nothing. Lately, however, perhaps at least partly in response to my work, Bush and Co. have concocted a story that he was speaking in Tyler, Texas to the Rotary Club. The vice-president of the Rotary Club, Aubrey Irby, says that Bush was speaking when the bellhop came over and told him, that Kennedy was dead.[58]

Mr. Irby passed the information on to Mr. Wendell Cherry, who passed it on to Bush; who stopped his speech. Irby says that Bush explained that he thought a political speech, under the circumstances, was inappropriate; and then he sat down. As a would-be alibi proving Bush's innocence, there are at least three huge problems with this story.

The first is that it is inconceivable that Bush would not have remembered such an event; or that he would have left it out of his autobiography, since it shows what a fine and respectful fellow he is. If he didn't remember it sooner, or include it in his autobiography, it's clearly because it never happened.

The second huge problem with this story is that it couldn't possibly have happened; that is, it

---

58 Kitty Kelley, The Family: the Real Story of the Bush Dynasty

is made impossible by Bush's original alibi, his phone call to the FBI, as you'll see. The witness who tells this story, Aubrey Irby, says that Bush excused himself and sat down. It doesn't say that he rushed out of the room in a frantic search for a phone. The problem is that Walter Cronkite's announcement to the world that Kennedy was dead came at 1:38 PM. Certainly, no one was listening to Walter Cronkite in the same room in which Bush was speaking. Therefore we can be sure that this bellhop, who told Irby that Kennedy was dead, was in another room. The bellhop had to make the decision that he had heard enough of the news to leave off listening to the news.

This is no small point. Texas governor Connally was severely wounded. Lyndon Johnson was reportedly wounded. There was much other news to be confirmed. At some point, then, the bellhop decided to stop listening and go make an announcement. There's no reason to think Irby would be the first person he would tell. But at some point he went to the room where Bush was speaking and informed Mr. Irby that the president was dead. This walk to find Irby took time, of course. Mr. Irby had to receive the information, and then he had to decide to inform Mr. Wendell Cherry, the president of the Kiwanis.

Mr. Cherry had to decide that he should interrupt Bush's speech; Mr. Cherry had to then walk over to Bush and tell him the news. Bush had to decide what to say; and he had to say it. And, according to the only witness, Mr. Irby, Bush "then sat down". Somehow, when he was finished sitting, without attracting Mr. Irby's attention, Bush had to seek and find a phone. This would have been a hotel phone, so he would likely have had to go through the hotel switchboard to get an outside line. Do you suppose the switchboard was busy after the announcement of the President's death? It's a good guess. In Washington D.C. so many people rushed to make a phone call that the phone system went down. In any case, once he got through to the hotel operator and got an outside line, Bush then had to call information and get the number of the FBI. After getting through to information, and getting the number, he then had to call the FBI; and penetrate their switchboard, which was, no doubt, very busy; and he had to locate an agent, on what must have been the busiest day in the history of the Dallas bureau. How many minutes do you suppose that would take? Twenty seems a fair guess, though it seems implausible that a civilian could even get through, given all the official police business going on at the time.

We know that the Dallas FBI was all over the murder scene, confiscating camera film and intimidating witnesses; so it's hard to imagine how Bush, an hour after the shooting, was able to reach an agent at all. Given the "sitting" that Mr. Irby observed Bush doing, for all this to have transpired in 45 minutes would be tidy work. But Bush had to do all of this, as the FBI memo states, by 1:45, seven minutes after the news of Kennedy's death first went out; which is blatantly impossible. The third problem is this question of why Bush would feel that it was necessary to concoct such a story at all? Why does he have to tell us this lie? Why does he have to get others, like Irby, to lie for him? The irony is that the harder he tries to make himself appear innocent, by lying, the more evidence he gives us of his guilt.

There are some people who manage to point to this and say "ahah! That's why Bush was in Dallas! Not to kill the President, but to speak to the other oilmen!" But as the Hoover memo shows, being an oilman was just a cover for Bush's real occupation as a CIA supervisor of trained killers. He needed an excuse for being in Dallas. This speaking engagement provided him with one.

20—Section 1   The Dallas Morning News.   Wednesday, November 20, 1963••••

CLUB ACTIVITIES

AMERICAN ASSOCIATION OF OILWELL DRILLING CONTRAC-TORS, 6:30 p.m. Thursday, Shera-ton-Dallas Hotel; George Bush, president, Zapata Off-Shore Co.

The Dallas Morning News, Wednesday, November 20, 1963, announces George H. W. Bush as the speaker for a meeting of the American Association of Oilwell Drilling Contractors on Thursday, November 21—the night before the assassination of JFK.

George Bush killed Kennedy. Or was it the Mafia? Maybe Castro did it. Who cares? It was 40 years ago. *What difference does it make? It matters.*

The day he died we lost an invaluable treasure. This video documents that we lost a man of peace, who tried to cool off the cold war, and to get the American people to see their Russian enemies, not as despicable inhuman monsters, but as people like us. On November 22, 1963, you lost the man who saved your life on October 17, 1962. At the height of the missile crisis, Kennedy's generals and advisors were urging him to launch a first strike attack against Cuba. They assured Kennedy that the Russian missiles in Cuba were not nuclear and were not ready; but that he and they should quietly slip away to the safety of bomb shelters anyway, just to be safe; and then launch an attack, leaving the rest of us out to die. Kennedy thought about it. And then he told them that nobody was going anywhere. If anyone died, they would be the first to go, sitting as they were in the Whitehouse, the prime target of those Russian missiles. Together they then figured out a safer plan. Robert McNamara, Secretary of Defense at the time, recently learned from the Russians that the missiles were armed, were ready, were nuclear, and that their commanders were authorized to use them in case of an attack. If you live in the northern hemisphere, the lives of your parents, and your future, were certainly saved by John Kennedy on that day. It matters that his killers be exposed.

In his farewell address, President Eisenhower had warned Kennedy, and the rest of us, of the threat posed to democracy by what Eisenhower called "the military industrial complex." And while Kennedy famously went after the CIA, and refused to commit troops to Vietnam, I always wondered why he didn't more openly attack this military industrial complex. And then I stumbled upon a speech he gave at the United Nations. As you will see in the video, he called upon the Russians, and United Nations, to help him to take on this military industrial complex, in order to "abolish all armies and all weapons." But he was swept away. And in the years since, millions have died in needless wars, trillions of dollars have been wasted on "defense", and millions more people have lived and died needlessly in poverty. It matters that we lost him.

In 2007, Bruce Willis told Vanity Fair magazine: "They still haven't caught the guy that killed Kennedy. I'll get killed for saying this, but I'm pretty sure those guys are still in power, in some form. The entire government of the United States was co-opted." Now Willis probably would not mind my suggesting that he's no genius. At best, his observation is common sense. 80% of the American people agree with him. Indeed, this video, proving that Kennedy was brought down by the most powerful men in the world and their hired thugs, is not based on secret documents.

It is all information that has merely been suppressed. Oswald allegedly shot Kennedy from behind. But the day he died, the NY Times carried the story, told by the doctors in Dallas, that Kennedy had an entrance wound in his throat, another in his right temple, and a large gaping exit wound in the back of his head. After talking to the emergency room doctors, Kennedy's press secretary described, to the assembled press, a shot to the right temple from the right front that went "right through the head."

All of the witnesses near the right front, the grassy knoll, described hearing shots from that direction, and dozens of witnesses raced up the knoll in pursuit of the shooters. These witnesses talked to the press. But all of this information has been suppressed for the last 50 years. By whom? Who could?

You will also see in this video the overwhelming best evidence, from the best witnesses, proving beyond a reasonable dispute, that Kennedy's body was stolen from Air Force One, and the wound to his right temple was mutilated, before the autopsy. Jackie Kennedy kept watch over an empty casket on the flight from Dallas to Bethesda Naval Hospital. Then the body was quietly taken to Bethesda for the autopsy, arriving 20 minutes before Jackie and the empty casket. Who had the power to arrange this?

Jacqueline Kennedy
first among all America's First Ladies
for coping with a pathetically unfaithful husband
who did not hesitate to take five bullets
for the sake of a free US

Who HAS the power today to suppress all this evidence?, and to continue to bombard us with ridiculous lies about a lone gunman? It's a short list, isn't it? It doesn't include the mafia, or the Russians, or Castro. It does include the Bush family – or rather their masters in Big Oil; the banking elite; the backbone of the military industrial complex. These men, and their successors, carried out the attacks of 9-11. It matters.

Operation Northwoods

In the covert war against the communist regime in Cuba under the CIA's Operation Mongoose, the U.S. Joint Chiefs of Staff unanimously proposed state-sponsored acts of terrorism inside the United States.

The plan included shooting down hijacked American airplanes, the sinking of U.S. ships, and the shooting of Americans on the streets of Washington, D.C. The outrageous plan even included a staged NASA disaster that would claim the life of astronaut John Glenn. Reeling under the embarrassing failure of the CIA's botched Bay of Pigs invasion of Cuba, president Kennedy rejected the plan in March of 1962. A few months later, Kennedy denied the plan's author, General Lyman Lemnitzer, a second term as the nation's highest ranking military officer.

In November of 1963, Kennedy was assassinated in Dallas, Texas.

"Dark Legacy" Documentary

Relying exclusively on government documents, statements from the best witnesses available, and the words from the mouths of the killers themselves, Dark Legacy produces a thoroughly substantiated criminal indictment of George Herbert Walker Bush, establishing beyond a reasonable doubt his guilt as a CIA supervisor in the conspiracy to assassinate John F. Kennedy. If this evidence would be presented to a jury in Texas, he would pay with his life.

Part one [of the documentary] presents the overwhelming mountain of evidence that President Kennedy was hit by bullets from the front and rear. Every witness in the Dallas emergency room attests, on camera, to the fact that a bullet from the right front blew a fist-sized hole in the back of the President's head. The New York Times carried these statements on the day of the murder; and has covered them up ever since.

Part two presents the on-camera testimony of the witnesses who actually handled the President's body, the FBI report, and the photographic evidence all proving unequivocally that the President's body was stolen from the Secret Service and the wounds altered, before the body was delivered to Bethesda Naval hospital for the autopsy. Jackie Kennedy accompanied an empty casket on the plane flight home. Who had the power to do all this without attracting public attention? It's a short list.

Part three presents the Nazi-connections of the Bush family, which prompted the FBI to seize their assets during WW II, as Nazi assets. It presents the suppressed fact that Watergate burglar and CIA operative E. Howard Hunt was found by a jury to have been in Dallas and involved in the conspiracy to kill Kennedy. Hunt was a supervisor of the misguided CIA-led anti-Castro Cubans who broke into the Watergate. He is not only connected to Bush through Watergate; and through Bush's father, Prescott; but five days after the assassination, the head of the FBI, J. Edgar Hoover, wrote a memo, titled "Assassination of President John Fitzgerald Kennedy" in which he named "George Bush of the Central Intelligence Agency" as the supervisor of what Hoover himself called the "misguided anti-Castro Cuban" killers of the President. Bush has said he doesn't remember the events of that day, but FBI documents place him in Dallas. It is difficult to assess the stature and significance of someone who has been dead as long as John Kennedy. His killers have also been his detractors, actively desecrating his memory, as they did his body. The movie begins with a short presentation of some of his most powerful and important speeches; including a stunning speech to the UN in which Kennedy calls for the complete abolition of the military industrial complex. These same men the military industrial complex, ripped him from us, and the darkest features of our history since that time are all directly the result of his murder. What will happen when the American people, and those of other Western nations, emerge from their cocoon of denial and face the reality that their rulers are among the worst criminals in human history?

Will the people follow their leaders' example and lapse into lawless, psychopathic behavior? Will Western leaders "flee forward" by launching wars designed to conceal the bloody tracks linking them to past misdeeds? Or will the pathocracy be overthrown and replaced by something more humane?

On such questions hinges the future of humanity. Given the high stakes, you would have to be crazy not to help spread the truth, change the system, and save the planet.

The Assassination of America

Another documentary whose purpose is to present the publicly unavailable and even suppressed historical audio, video, and film recordings largely unseen by the American public relating to the assassination of the Kennedy brothers, is a 10-hours long documentary series named Evidence of Revision: The Assassination of America. You can see it here.

It also details the little known classified Black Ops actually used to intentionally create the massive war in Viet Nam, the CIA "mind control" programs and their involvement in the RFK assassination and the Jonestown massacre and other important truths of our post-modern time.

EPILOGUE
One Motive, One Initiator

E.1 The Four Chapters

All testimonies selected in the Chapters are offered by first-hand witnesses, or describe them. I see no reason to doubt any of them, except when they speak out their own opinion. In this Section I will speak out mine. As hopefully clarified in the Introduction to this book, I do not base myself on a single, clearly coherent set of historical facts. I view the four murders as a single coherent set of historical facts. After reading this chapter, the reader can judge by him or herself what the odds are that I am justified in doing so. *To ease your minds: LBJ, GWH Bush, US mobs, Texas oil and mining magnates, are all **not** initiator/mind/coordinator of JFK's assassination: they were mere tools in the hands of the Client.*

What emerges in the **first Chapter**, is a long chain of misinformation: a clear pointer to self-hiding by the Client, just like illegal corporations do when using an impenetrable network of bank accounts of shareholder companies in countries all over the globe. If Oswald's lone wolf theory were true, why would it be followed up by so much ado about seemingly connected people? Such a series of events is simply the evolution of a public-versus-initiator debate between the lines: the public expresses indignation concerning some fact, the initiator responds by having commissioners leak information to the press, again the public responds, and so forth.

In the sections of that chapter, there is the irrefutable acoustic study by Robertson, who synchronized Zapruder's silent video footage with McLain's loose "DictaBelt" noise tape. Specifically important are the "revelations" that the *forward motion of JFK's head obviously corresponds to a shot from behind* (either from the Texas School Book Depository, or from the Dal-Tex building, whose extremes both have a full sight over the Elm Street, from Houston Street until the triple underpass) and his subsequent *backward motion obviously corresponds to a shot from the front* (either from the Grassy Knoll, or from the triple overpass). This book shows only four frames from the Zapruder video footage. However, everyone can see the full footage on youtube, and convince oneself that the backward motion of the Presidents head, torn out of Jackie's embrace, displaces by one full meter in a fraction of a second. One does not need to be an astronaut to understand what that means, physically. It means that JFK's head exploded on taking the bullet. The bullet carried the momentum necessary to cause the President head's initial displacement velocity. In ordinary high-school physics tis is called "momentum conservation": Bullet mass times bullet velocity plus head mass times head velocity is constant. Hence, Robertson's study confirms, in a very scientific way, what all mentally sane physicists can deduce by merely seeing the Zapruder video. *Every possible negation is due to either plain insanity or commissioning by "the Client" (equals initiator equals mental author of the assassination).*

The conclusion that nothing is wrong with Jack Ruby's mental capabilities is equally plain from the second section. The fact that his own lawyers try everything to silence him, until shouting out that he's insane, only corroborates the conspiracy view. Insane are rather people *who do not see this, when fully informed.* Of course such Americans exist: but statistically, not a fraction more than fools exist in other countries around the globe.

The fake movements by President Trump, mentioned in the third section, only add the information that the Client has the power to make Trump dance at his tune.

In the fourth section there is a full testimony of someone who still loves LBJ, as her best friend in life, yet does not refrain from telling the truth, even when this sheds some dark light on her lover. What more credits does the US need to consider such a testimony truthful? Possibly an HSCA report of two thousand pages? Else, the conclusion is simple: LBJ was delirious with the briefing, but he was certainly not the initiator. At Murchison's estate, only one commissioner did the talking, and all others were silent, either to be informed (like all Texas banking, weapons, oil and mining business elite, the old Murchison included), or to confirm the information (like the two mafia bosses, and CIA people).

The fifth section leaves no doubt as to the participation of an ultra-high-tech photography laboratory in producing Life journal's artifact front page. Who seeks a single initiator of all these sections' occurrences, automatically implies a degree of coincidence that vanishes with respect to the probability of life starting on earth, according to Hoyle's still non-debunked calculations concerning the origin of life. Let the fools believe in such lame odds (once in 10 billion years); you do not need to.

The sixth section reports the real head wound forensics, instead of the framed ones showing but a single throat shot. How can such a wound alone explain that motorcade officers, ordered to keep their distance from the limousine (obviously to allow the snipers a clear shot) had to wipe rests of JKF's brains off their clothes and gloves? How does that explain the burst of blood and brain matter swirled into the air in the Zapruder video?

The last three sections discuss several dismantled efforts by the Client to cover up his existence. India exists, mister Client. Even though I do not see it right now, below my feet, or in the far distance. I do not need to see your picture to deduce rationally, from the historical facts, that you do exist. Just like all the Jews in WW II knew that Hitler existed, although nobody ever saw him directly.

The **second Chapter** leaves no doubt that Mr. Client obviously had to make any trustful declarations about JFK's assassination impossible. He had no choice but killing Bobby, too. The only anxiety this chapter causes me, is that the Kennedy's might have totally underestimated the size of the Client. This anxiety is only magnified in the **third Chapter**, describing the political murder of Ted Kennedy. If he had really known the size of the Client, he would never have gone to Chappaquiddick with his mistress in the first place. What happened over there is so simple, that I do not understand I never saw it written: the Client had Ted intoxicated with a drug that reduced him to a walking zombie. Walking away from a deadly accident possibly provoked by himself? If you know a single other elected candidate for presidency in the US who behaves like Ted behaved after the accident, please let me know.

Now that all three politically active and credible siblings had been assassinated, one would think all loose threads were dealt with. But surprise, surprise, suddenly John-John enters the scene in the **fourth Chapter**, and in but a single stroke, he

(i)   proves Rabin's murder to be ordered by Israeli secret Services (at least three of them)
(ii) communicates through the lines that George WH Bush and his CIA played a key role in assassinating his father, and
(iii) promises a research into a related aspect.

Too bad, however, that neither your father, nor your mother, nor a single Kennedy for that, had an idea of the Client's size. A few weeks later you were picked up, lifeless, from the sea surface. By now, the great public got used to the "Kennedy Curse", a word combination invented by the Client, which poor drugged Ted used against himself.

Is everything said by now? Not at all, dear reader, please bear with me a few more pages. I still owe you the name of the gunman of the eighth and decisive shot, and that of the Client.

E.2 The Eigth Shot

Before directing his historical legal-conspiracy thriller Oliver Stone tried to interview James Files, but was refused three times, "because Files did not like him". Although Stone's production lacks Files' crucial information, it contains many correct intuitions. Lee Harvey Oswald was a CIA field official. His own Agency used him as a patsy (nice place to work, the CIA).

James Files (aka Sutton), a genuine hit man and responsible for the fifth bullet, exploding JFK's brains, is the only mob survivor, because in prison he never talked. His three colleagues, James John Rosselli, who shot the president in the neck, and their sub-bosses Charles Nicoletti and Sam Giancana, were all executed in the 1970's. Below a short fragment of Files' confession on his scouting cooperation with Lee Harvey Oswald, shortly before his boss informed him on his definitive assignment: to fire a lead-filled (exploding-upon contact) bullet from the Grassy Knoll through the left eye[59] of JFK.

> "Lee Harvey Oswald knew that I was there but I never told him why I was there. He had just been come over and told to stay with me and to help me out and to assist in any way he could. Lee Harvey Oswald and I never discussed the assassination of John F. Kennedy. I discussed

---

59 As Files' position was on the Grassy Knoll, his shot would necessarily hit the President from the left. The President's left eye was simply the horizontal center of Files' vision of JFK's head at brain height.

that with no one. Because my part of it... I had no part of the assassination at that time... all I did was go down, take the car down, take the weapons down, clean the weapons, calibrate the scopes, make sure everything was functioning properly and then know the immediate area surrounding Dealey Plaza back to the expressways and the other local highways that could be used as an extraction point to leave Dallas in case something should go wrong. At that point, I had no involvement at all in the assassination outside of that... just doing my little job that I had to do."

This is the way hit men talk: like a computer, incapable of moral restraints. Extensive details can be found in the book *Files on JFK* by Wim Dankbaar.[60] Wikipedia's page on the "CIA Kennedy assassination conspiracy theory" is in complete contradiction with Wim Dankbaar's findings; obviously, the page was written by a government official and ordered by the Client. Nearly all of Wikipedia's pages concerning conspiracy theories are Client-ordered, a happy exception being the Mineta page.

Interestingly, James Files revealed that he filled his only bullet (as he was to take the last possible shot) with lead because of its explosive effect upon impact. Obviously, the Congress will never allow an independent chemical analysis of the president's remains, which are full of lead: the Client will never let that happen.

---

60 BookSurge Publishing, December 2005

Wikipedia mentions that in his death bed, CIA Howard Hunt accused Lyndon B. Johnson of being responsible for Kennedy's assassination. Well thank you very much for this confession, Mr. Hunt, but you are much too late (LBJ could not respond anymore) and your accusations are far too much in line with the Client's endeavors to make them credible.

E.3 Max Leland

Senator Max Leland initially was part of the Warren Commission. When he openly declared the investigation was compromised due to multiple constraints on source accessibility,[61] he was replaced. Here, Cleland accuses the government of delaying or denying access to vital documents; note that his order was to report to Congress in May 27, 2004. In November 23, 2003, UPI announced that

> "the past Senator Max Cleland has been nominated to be a member of the Export-Import Band by President Bush. Therefore, he will have to abdicate the Commission that investigates the terrorist attacks of 11-S."

---

61 "If this decision stands, I, as a member of the commission, cannot look any American in the eye, especially family members of victims, and say the commission had full access. This investigation is now compromised", see http://www.oilempire.us/investigation.html

He was replaced by Senator Bob Kerrey, a war criminal and fan of PNAC (Project for the New American Century, a neoconservative think tank founded by Dick Cheney in 1997). When too much rumor concerning CIA involvement in Kennedy's assassination circulated, President Lyndon B. Johnson appointed John J. McCloy[62] as a member of the Warren Commission, with the obvious objective of preventing any further research of the CIA. If Americans had known that George W.H. Bush was heading the CIA at that time, and was arrested for suspicious behavior on Dealey Plaza, THE CLIENT would need another patsy to deviate the attention. This allegation is quite widespread (see e.g. Joan Didion's „Miami") and confirms that the Warren Commission was instituted in order to cover up the CIA as the origin of the assassination. Other examples of specific expertise needed to cover up THE CLIENT: ex-CIA director and member of the Commission Allan Dulles personally supervised all hearings of CIA and FBI officials, making sure nothing compromising would issue from there.

The official 889-page report made public on September 27th 1964 concluded what any conspiracy would have done, namely, that Lee Harvey Oswald and Jack Ruby both had actuated on their own. Thank you, Warren Commission, for this ulterior proof of your being but everything but a Research Commission. The Warren report went straight into the bin when some 50 years later

---

62 John J. McCloy was former president of the World Bank and of the Chase Manhattan Bank, former chairman of the Council on Foreign Relations, former trustee of the Rockefeller foundation, former chairman of the Ford Foundation, yet all but a homicide investigator.

(2013) CIA-historian David Robarge wrote, with solid proof, that McCone and other CIA agents had withheld crucial information „for the good of America". Robarge's story does not tell the truth either, of course. It simply abuses of the fact that McCone, who died in 1991, could not defend himself anymore. Everything goes, as long as it helps erasing the Client's trails.

In 1976 the Congress established the House Select Committee on Assassinations (HSCA) for rehabilitating the heavily damaged Warren Commission. HSCA declared the validity of Kantor's testimony, which the Warren Commission had previously confuted. Their 1979 Final Report reads:

> Ruby's shooting of Oswald was not a spontaneous act, in that it involved at least some premeditation. Similarly, the committee believed it was less likely that Ruby entered the police basement without assistance, even though the assistance may have been provided with no knowledge of Ruby's intentions... The committee was troubled by the apparently unlocked doors along the stairway route and the removal of security guards from the area of the garage nearest the stairway shortly before the shooting... There is also evidence that the Dallas Police Department withheld relevant information from the Warren Commission concerning Ruby's entry to the scene of the Oswald transfer.

These sentences shout out "conspiracy", without mentioning the word itself.

E.4 Gerald Ford's perjury in written

Gerald R. Ford changed ever so slightly the Warren Commission's main sentence on the place where a bullet entered President John F. Kennedy's body. Mr. Ford's change strengthened the Warren conclusion that a single bullet entered through Kennedy's neck, exited through his throat, again entered and exited Gov. John B. Connally's body, in order to finally bounce off the car and explode the president's brains — a crucial element in the Warren deduction that Lee Harvey Oswald was the sole gunman. Mr. Ford, who was a member of the commission, wanted a change to show that the bullet entered Kennedy "at the back of his neck" rather than in his uppermost back, as the commission originally wrote. After Dankbaar had demonstrated the Warren report was but a pile of lies, *Mr. Ford was so kind to stipulate, "I intended the change in order to clarify meaning, not to alter history"*. I literally fell off my chair from a burst of laughter upon reading this silly comment. Poor America — if this characterizes the moral integrity of your presidents you are one hundred yards below sea level.

E.5 Kennedy's EO 11,110

We finally come to the real cause of Kennedy's death. Not his AUW speech, not his "failure" in the Bay of Pigs, not his "weakness" during the Cuba missile crisis, not his firing Earle Cabell's brother from the CIA Deputy Directorship, not his intentionally humiliating LBJ, not his being anti-tycoon, whether in the oil, mining, or weapons business. Not his being a bad President. Not even all these reasons together!

So what was JFK's mortal sin?

On June 4, 1963, President John F. Kennedy signed a decree with the authority to strip the Federal Bank of its power to print money, and to loan it to the United States Federal Government at interest. With the stroke of a pen, Kennedy declared that the privately owned Federal Reserve Bank would soon be out of business. The Christian Law Fellowship has exhaustively researched this matter through the Federal Register and Library of Congress. One may safely conclude the absence of any subsequent Executive Order repealing, amending, or superseding Executive Order 11,110. In simple terms, it is still valid. By signing this EO, JFK returned the currency printing rights to where they truly belong: in the hands of the US Federal Government, voted by the American People.

President Kennedy's Executive Order 11,110 gave the Treasury Department the explicit authority: "to issue silver certificates against any silver bullion, silver, or standard silver dollars in the Treasury." This means that for every ounce of silver in the US Treasury's vault, the government could introduce new money into circulation based on the silver bullion physically held there. US Treasury brought more than $4 billion United States Notes into circulation in $2 and $5 denominations. $10 and $20 United States Notes never circulated but the Treasury Department was printing them the very day of Kennedy's assassination.

US Treasury issued "United States Notes" as an interest-free and debt-free currency backed by its silver reserves. The "Federal Reserve Note" issued from the private central bank of the US (the Federal Reserve Bank, also known as Federal Reserve System) looks almost like a "United States Note" from the US Treasury issued by President Kennedy's Executive Order, except one says "Federal Reserve Note" on the top while the other says "United States Note".

Most importantly, the FED started taking out of circulation all United States Notes the very day of the president's assassination. Federal Reserve Notes continued to serve as the legal currency of the nation. According to the United States Secret Service, 99% of all US paper "currency" circulating in 1999 are Federal Reserve Notes. Kennedy knew that if the silver-backed United States Notes were widely circulated, they would have eliminated the demand for Federal Reserve Notes. This is a very simple matter of economics. The USN were backed by silver, while the FRN by nothing. Executive Order 11,110 should have prevented the national debt from reaching its current level (virtually all of the nearly $9 trillion in federal debt has been created since 1963) if Lyndon Johnson or any subsequent President were to enforce it. Of course LBJ did not do it himself, as he owed his new job to the Client, who appeared to have a really strong connection with the FED.

Aha! That is where it hurts: JFK had dared to challenge Mr. Rothschild's banking empire, which includes a large majority of the FED and its associates, and a large majority of all European banks. Such huge size of the Client JFK was not able to imagine, in spite of his holding the highest possible public office in the US.

In order to keep his FED business alive, Rothschild had to sacrifice the three brothers Jack, Bobby, and Ted, plus Jack's son John-John. Luckily enough for the present Kennedy, no one seems to be politically dangerous for EZ. If so, they will be killed by EZ, too. For a proof of this last statement I refer my dear reader to Yitzhak Q. Rosenthal's masterpiece "The Snake".

E.6 EZ's Second Secret Service

From the behavior of Bush senior on Dealey Plaza, the day that President Kennedy was assassinated, it is obvious that the CIA was deeply implicated in the whole operation. Who still believe the story of bullets bouncing off a car multiple times, or lone wolf Lee Harvey Oswald busying himself with selfies, armed with the rifle he will be using to shoot down JFK, should take a glance at the book "patriotic ingenuousness".

So let us return to reality. US' Central Intelligence Agency is EZ's "less invisible" secret service. EZ does not "own" the CIA, but, part of it offers regular services to EZ, in return for big money of course. EZ does own its fully dedicated, "more invisible" Secret Service: the Israeli Mossad.

Mossad is a short for *HaMossad leModiʿin ule-Tafkidim Meyuḥadim*, meaning "Institute for Intelligence and Special Operations". It is the national intelligence agency of Israel and one of the main entities in the Israeli Intelligence Community, along with Aman (military intelligence) and Shin Bet (internal security).[63]

Mossad is responsible for intelligence collection, covert operations, and counterterrorism. Mossad is separate from Israel's democratic institutions. Because no law defines its purpose, objectives, roles, missions, powers or budget and because it is exempt from the constitutional laws of the State of Israel Mossad has been described as a deep state. Its director answers directly and only to the Prime Minister. It's annual budget is estimated to be around 10 billion shekels (US$2.73 billion) and it is estimated that it employs around 7,000 people directly, making it the second-largest espionage agency in the Western world, after the American CIA.

Mossad was formed on December 13, 1949, as the Central Institute for Coordination at the recommendation of Prime Minister David Ben-Gurion to Reuven Shiloah. Ben Gurion wanted a central body to coordinate and improve cooperation between the existing security services—the army's intelligence department (Aman), the Internal Security Service (Shin Bet), and the foreign office's "political department". In March 1951, it was reorganized and made a

---

63 https://en.wikipedia.org/wiki/Mossad

part of the prime minister's office, reporting directly to the prime minister.

Mossad's Counter-terrorist units are

- *Metsada*, a unit responsible for attacking the enemy. It runs "small units of combatants" whose missions include "assassinations and sabotage".
- *Kidon*, a unit which belongs to the Caesarea department (one of Mossad's eight departments). It is described by Yaakov Katz as "an elite group of expert assassins who operate under the Caesarea branch of the espionage organization. Not much is known about this mysterious unit, details of which are some of the most closely guarded secrets in the Israeli intelligence community." It recruits from "former soldiers from the elite IDF special force units."
- *IDF* has been a part of Israel's policy of assassinations, which according to Ronen Bergman is a policy that Israel has used more than any other country in the West since world war II, stating it has carried out at least 2,700 assassination missions.

Mossad has opened a venture capital fund, in order to invest in hi-tech startups to develop new cyber technologies. The names of technology startups funded by Mossad will not be published. Together with Shurat HaDin, they started Operation Harpoon, for "destroying terrorists' money networks."

Until here the Wikipedia quote.

The original motto of the Israeli Secret Service Mossad reads (Mishle 24:6)

"For by *tachbulot* thou shalt wage thy *milchamah*, and in a multitude of *yo'etz* there is *teshu'ah*."

The untranslated Hebrew words literally mean

Tachbulot:	wise guidance
Milchamah:	war
Yo'etz:	counselors
Teshu'ah:	victory

The Catholic interpretation of Proverbs 24:6 is

Tachbulot:	spiritual guidance
Milchamah:	ascetic self-control
Yo'etz:	spiritual counselors
Teshu'ah:	inner peace

Mossad's interpretation of Proverbs 24:6 is

Tachbulot:	deceit
Milchamah:	submission of all heathens
Yo'etz:	secret international network
Teshu'ah:	victory of God's elected people

E.7 Rowing with the Oars You Happen to Have

The title of this subsection is a direct translation of a Dutch saying. If it does not exist in English, the meaning is obvious: one should try to reach one's goal with whatever tools one happens to have.

Since EZ does not "own" the CIA, and much less "owns" the American people's free minds, EZ is quite limited in its possibilities. One of their worst moments occurred in 2015 in London, when the Israeli and English Secret Services got into a public fight over who had ordered the underground bombings. Genius Benjamin Netanyahu did not really offer the best service to EZ by publicly claiming that he was alerted by Mossad for the bombings a quarter of an hour before his leaving the hotel for the conference.

Probably, Netanyahu was instructed to say this by his very Mossad, who initially tried to blame Muslim terrorists for trying to assassinate the Israeli Prime Minister. But English Secret Services are less malleable than the near-idiotic Swedish, Spanish, Dutch, French, or German ones, to name but a few. Scotland Yard hit back harshly and made the Mossad look like a bunch of amateurs.

This intrinsic limitation to EZ's warfare has a major consequence: they always rely on a single pattern. The latter contains the following ingredients:

- Before attacking a country, blame it by a one-year publicity campaign for producing the nerve gas (e.g. Sarin) Mossad will be using. In the aftermath, prove your point by taking NATO-supervised samples of air contamination. If there indeed are traces of Sarin, the enemy (in Israel's case: Iraq, Syria, Russia, and, after Trump's term, Iran) is guilty.

- Filling the Venture Capital of Mossad is not that easy. The best direct way to do so, is to scare Americans and Europeans (the rich countries, in general) for "Muslim terror". I put these words in quote signs because Muslim terror hardly exists. All Muslim terror groups, that do exist, are financed by EZ and execute their orders. For these Muslim youngsters living in extreme poverty, this is just a way to make a living. From time to time, in order to make them believe that they really fight for a Muslim cause, EZ plans a "Muslim attack" in Israel. It has the added value that no Israeli will ask any questions regarding their Secret Services: for without them, it simply would be much worse. So tell me, dear reader: how difficult is it for EZ to keep Gaza in permanent war with Israel?

- Before 9/11, Americans were against raising the yearly Defense budget. After 9/11, the Americans wanted nothing but that. The same happens in Europe, particularly in France, as that is the country that best succeeded in integrating Muslims. Hence, in France most political gain is to be won by faking Muslim terrorist attacks.

- Stupid mistakes in the execution of a fake terrorist attack, like dumping the wrong plane engine close to the Twin Towers, are inevitable. This is simply because EZ is not allowed to leave a single trace of their presence. Although the plan is perfect, the execution always depends on partially misinformed mercenaries.

- EZ turns all such mistakes into their own profit. First, mistakes explode the number of well-meant conspiracy theories, that is, those proposed by the independent-thinking elite of the suffering country. Second, these mistakes allow EZ to bring plenty of their own misleading conspiracy theories on the market, in order to discredit conspiracy theories for being what they are: conspiracy theories.

- Consequently, the sleeping part of a country's people believe the official government's account, which is ten times worse than any non-EZ produced account. For the sleepers: one can tell an EZ conspiracy theory from a non-EZ conspiracy theory by the time it survives on the web.

E8. The Client

The Client's name is Jacob Rothschild.
His motive is the seizure of universal (financial) power.

Nikkolò calls Rothschild's criminal organization
"Extreme Zionism" (EZ), throughout the decalogue.

Suggested Further Reading

Yitzhak Q. Rosenthal, "The Snake" (2019)

Juleon Schins, "Patriotic Ingenuousness" (2019)

Niccolò, "Beginner's Guide to the FED" (2019)